LONGMAN HISTORY PROJECT

General Editor: Josh Brooman

Germany 1918–45: Democracy and Dictatorship

JOSH BROOMAN

LONGMAN

Addison Wesley Longman Limited
Edinburgh Gate, Harlow, Essex CM20 2JE, England and
Associated Companies throughout the World.

First published 1996
Fourth impression 1997
ISBN 0 582 28809 6

The right of Josh Brooman to be identified as author of this work has been
asserted by him in accordance with Copyright, Designs and Patents Act 1988.

Set in Concorde and Tekton

Produced by Hart McLeod

Produced by Longman Asia Limited, Hong Kong.
SWTC/04

The Publisher's policy is to use paper manufactured from sustainable forests.

Illustrations by Sheila Betts and Josh Brooman.

Cover photograph: a group of schoolgirls being evacuated from Vienna in
September 1939.

Acknowledgements

We are grateful to the following for permission to reproduce photographs and
other copyright material:

AKG London, pages 25, 33, 52, 79; Archiv Gerstenberg, page 11; Bildarchiv
Preussischer Kulturbesitz, pages 12 centre, 47, 50, 87; Bundesarchiv, pages 36,
43, 44, 61, 65, 91, 95, 100, 103, 107; Deutsches Historisches Museum, Berlin,
page 4-5; E.T Archive, page 105; Heinrich R. Hoffmann, page 55; Hulton-
Deutsch Collection, page 12 left; Robert Hunt Library, pages 10, 68, 73; Imperial
War Museum, London, pages 77, 97, 117, 124; Jewish Historical Institute, page
112 (photo: Wiener Library); David King Collection, page 16; Beate Klarsfeld
Foundation, page 113 (photo: Wiener Library); Landesarchiv, Berlin, page 20;
Library of Congress, page 106; Ruth Liepman Agency, page 120 (photo; Wiener
Library); Panstwowe Museum, Poland, page 114; Range/Bettmann/UPI, page 31;
Suddeutscher Verlage, pages 41, 54, 56 above left, above right & below right, 62,
63, 72, 102; Sygma, pages 56 below left (L'Illustration), 70 (Keystone), 115
(Keystone, Paris); Topham Picturepoint, page 12 right; US Army Center of
Military History, page 89; Ullstein Bilderdienst, page 8, 21, 24 right, 38, 40, 42,
58, 75, 81, 85, 99, 101, 118; Weimar Archive, page 53; Wiener Library, pages 24
centre, 57, 66, 76, 93. We are unable to trace the copyright holders of the
following and would be grateful for any information that would enable us to do
so: pages 15, 17, 24 left, 29, 59, 80, 92 & 96 & 116 (photo supplied by
Cambridge University Library), 119.

Contents

Unit 1 · An experiment in democracy: the Revolution of 1918–19

Look at this photograph. Something unusual is happening. Ordinary working people are marching along a street in Germany, carrying rifles. A man in a bow tie has a machine gun on a stolen lorry. Some soldiers are marching with them. The shops are shut. What is going on? Why have workers and soldiers taken to the streets with rifles?

The answer is that a revolution was taking place. These men were revolutionaries who wanted to change the way their country was run. Together with thousands like them, all over Germany, they overthrew their ruler and set up a new kind of government.

Their aim was to make Germany a democratic country. This means that the people would elect their government, have a say in how it runs the country, and have equal rights. But they disagreed about how to achieve this. For three months they argued and then fought each other in a civil war. Thousands were killed before a democratic government was set up in 1919.

Unit 1 of this book can be used to answer three questions. First, why did German people join a revolution in 1918–19? Second, why did the revolutionaries start fighting each other? And third, how did Germany change as a result of their revolution?

Striking workers and soldiers march along a street in Berlin, the capital of Germany, on 5 January 1919.

Germany before the Revolution

* **Kaiser**   The German word for Emperor. Like the Russian word 'Tsar', it came from the Latin word 'Caesar'.

Source 1

The German Empire, 1871–1918 – a union of Prussia with 25 neighbouring states, each ruled by a King, Duke or Prince. The King of Prussia was Kaiser (Emperor) of the 26 states.

The German Empire

Germany before 1918 was an empire in the centre of Europe. It was ruled by Kaiser* Wilhelm the Second. It was a young country, created in 1871, but was already one of the world's most powerful states. The map below (Source 1) shows its main features.

German government

The most powerful person in Germany was Kaiser Wilhelm. He was head of the government, appointing ministers to run the country. He was head of the civil service and commander of the armed forces. And he was the King of Prussia, largest of the 26 states in the Empire.

Although Kaiser Wilhelm had great power, Germany's government did have some democratic features. Men of 25 and over had the right to vote

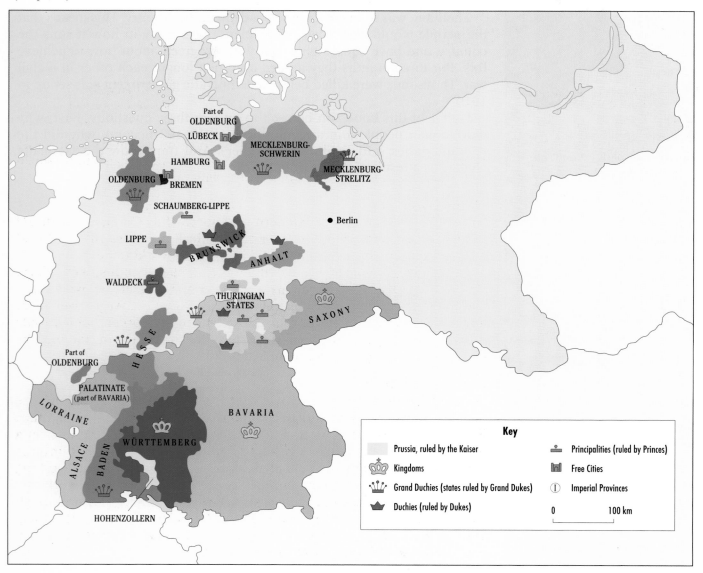

Part of OLDENBURG
LÜBECK
HAMBURG
MECKLENBURG-SCHWERIN
MECKLENBURG-STRELITZ
OLDENBURG
BREMEN
SCHAUMBERG-LIPPE
• Berlin
LIPPE
BRUNSWICK
ANHALT
WALDECK
THURINGIAN STATES
SAXONY
HESSE
Part of OLDENBURG
PALATINATE (part of BAVARIA)
LORRAINE
BAVARIA
ALSACE
BADEN
WÜRTTEMBERG
HOHENZOLLERN

Key

	Prussia, ruled by the Kaiser		Principalities (ruled by Princes)
	Kingdoms		Free Cities
	Grand Duchies (states ruled by Grand Dukes)	Ⓘ	Imperial Provinces
	Duchies (ruled by Dukes)		0 100 km

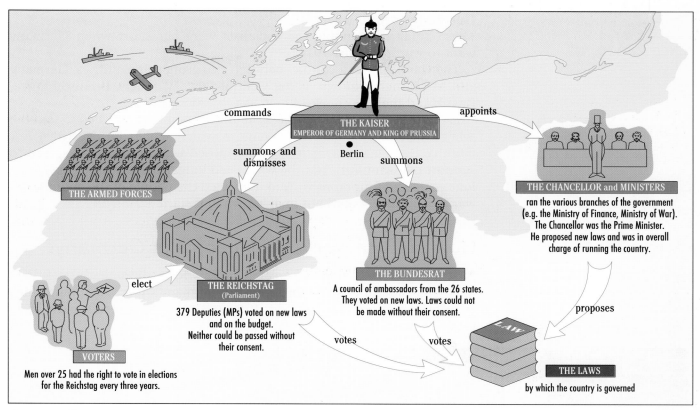

The following labels appear within the diagram:

commands

THE KAISER
EMPEROR OF GERMANY AND KING OF PRUSSIA

appoints

summons and dismisses

Berlin

summons

THE ARMED FORCES

THE CHANCELLOR and MINISTERS
ran the various branches of the government
(e.g. the Ministry of Finance, Ministry of War).
The Chancellor was the Prime Minister.
He proposed new laws and was in overall
charge of running the country.

elect

THE REICHSTAG
(Parliament)

379 Deputies (MPs) voted on new laws
and on the budget.
Neither could be passed without
their consent.

THE BUNDESRAT
A council of ambassadors from the 26 states.
They voted on new laws. Laws could not
be made without their consent.

proposes

votes   votes

VOTERS
Men over 25 had the right to vote in elections
for the Reichstag every three years.

LAW

THE LAWS
by which the country is governed

Source 2

How the German Empire was
governed before 1918.

for a parliament called the Reichstag. This voted on the laws which Kaiser Wilhelm and his ministers drew up. However, the Reichstag had no say in foreign or military affairs, nor in the choosing of ministers.

German industry

Germany's industries were modern and successful. Germany produced more iron and steel than any other country in Europe. Its output of coal matched that of Great Britain, as did its share of world trade.

As Germany's industries grew, so did the number of industrial workers. By 1914 over half of all Germans worked in mines, factories, workshops and transport. Many were unhappy with their situation. Wages were often low and working conditions bad. More and more workers joined trade unions, and supported socialist parties, in the hope of forcing the government to improve their conditions.

German socialists

Socialists wanted power and wealth to be shared equally among the people. However, they disagreed about the best way of doing this. Revolutionary socialists wanted to overthrow Germany's ruling class in a revolution. This would mean getting rid of the Kaiser, the Kings, Princes and Dukes, the landowners and all rich people. In their place, the working class would govern Germany through local, elected councils of workers.

In contrast, parliamentary socialists believed in winning power through parliament. If they could persuade Kaiser Wilhelm to give the Reichstag more power, they thought they could use the large number of votes they had to change the way Germany was governed.

Germany goes to war

These arguments among the socialists were cut short when Germany went to war in August 1914.

The war began as a conflict between two groups of countries. Germany and its partners (known as the Central Powers) fought Britain, France, Russia and their partners (known as the Allies).

At first there was great enthusiasm for the war. Men flocked to join the army, expecting it to be an adventure which would be over in a few months. Even many socialists, who opposed war on principle, agreed to support the war effort. But the war lasted longer than anyone expected – four years and four months. And it affected the people of the countries at war in ways they could not imagine when it started.

How did the war affect people in Germany?

First and foremost, the war created serious food shortages. The British navy blockaded the sea approaches to Germany's ports, stopping ships from bringing food and supplies from overseas. As a result, even basic foods were strictly rationed (see Source 3).

Source 3

A street in Berlin in 1917. Hungry crowds queue outside a Municipal Potato Store (Städtischer Kartoffel Verkauf) for potatoes being unloaded from the carts in the street.

The longer the war lasted, the more serious the shortages became. Source 4 gives us a clear idea of their severity:

The workers' menu of 1915 was:
1. Early morning lunch (5.45 a.m.): four slices of bread with butter or fresh lard, cheese or sausage, coffee.
2. Breakfast at 8.00 a.m: bread and cheese sandwich and coffee.
3. Noon meal: meat or fish, potatoes (any amount).
4. Supper: soup, meat or fish, potatoes, peas, rice or hominy*.

* **hominy** Cornmeal porridge.

Source 4

A propaganda leaflet, printed in German, which the British army dropped from balloons over German towns in summer 1918.

In April 1917 it was different:
1. Breakfast: two pieces of dried bread and potatoes.
2. Dinner: cooked beets one day, the next day cooked seaweed or beets and a few potatoes.

After the revolt of the German people, the Allies…will supply them with food and clothing…. But these will be withheld until the military authority in Germany collapses.

British secret agents in Germany sent reports back to Britain about the effects of the blockade on Germany. These reports revealed other shortages:

Source 5

The Foreign Office, *The Economic Situation in Germany and Austria-Hungary, 1914–1918,* Confidential Report no 11025, September 1918

…In addition to other hardships, the German public is threatened this winter with an almost complete lack of lights of every description: electric light, gas, lamp oil and candles. The lack of soap and washing powder makes personal cleanliness impossible and helps the spread of disease. Medicines are difficult to obtain…. In the industrial district of Westphalia many of the women have hardly any clothing and are going about in a thin blouse and skirt, bare legged with wooden shoes.

As living conditions grew worse, more and more workers protested by going on strike. The complaints of workers in Berlin can be seen in this newspaper report of a strike meeting held on 29 January 1918:

Source 6

Vorwärts ('Forwards' – the newspaper of the Social Democratic Party), 29 January 1918.

* **the right of assembly**
The right to organise or attend public meetings.

The meeting formulated the following demands:
- The speedy bringing about of peace….
- Better food supplies….
- The complete restoration of the right of assembly* as well as the right of free discussion….
- An end to military control of industries.
- The immediate release of all persons convicted or arrested for political action.
- The right to vote in the Prussian parliament for all men and women over 20 years old.

Questions

1 Look at Sources 3 and 4. What do they tell you about the effects of the war on the German people?

2 Read Source 5. Other than food, what shortages were caused by the war?

3 Source 6 shows six demands of workers in Berlin.
   a Which demands were to do with the war?
   b Which demands were about people's political rights?

4 Using the text and sources in this section, explain why many Germans in 1918 were unhappy with their government.

The Revolution of 1918

Conditions get worse

As winter approached in 1918, conditions grew much worse. Food supplies ran so low that most adults were living on less than 1,000 calories a day – starvation level. Fuel shortages led to power cuts, factory closures and transport problems. A killer strain of the flu virus swept across Germany, killing thousands of people each week. On the battle fronts, two of Germany's allies decided to stop fighting, while the German armies were forced to retreat.

Faced with this worsening situation at home, and with defeat on the battlefields, the German army decided to ask the Allies for peace.

An attempt at democracy

The Allies were prepared to make peace with Germany – but only on certain conditions. They said that Germany's government must be made more democratic before they would even start talking about peace. In other words, Kaiser Wilhelm must share his power.

On 2 October, Wilhelm did exactly that. He allowed the main parties in the Reichstag, Germany's parliament, to form a new government. Over the next three weeks, the new government took away many of the Kaiser's powers and gave them to the Reichstag.

But this change did not satisfy many people. Public opinion turned against the Kaiser (see Source 1). People blamed him for their worsening conditions and said he should give up his throne. Some talked of overthrowing him in a revolution.

Source 1

This cartoon was drawn in 1918 by the German artist Raemaeker. It shows Kaiser Wilhelm (centre) hand in hand with war (on the left) and starvation (on the right).

Source 2

Mutiny in the German navy. These sailors have taken control of their warships in Wilhelmshaven, at the start of November 1918. They have unloaded ammunition (left) from the ships.

Mutiny in the navy

A revolution began on 28 October when Germany's navy chiefs made an unpopular decision. They ordered the warships in Kiel harbour to put to sea. Their aim was to fight the British navy for control of the sea between Britain and Europe.

Sailors on the ships were horrified by the order. They knew that peace talks had begun and that the war might soon be over. They said it would be suicide to fight the British, and refused to obey the order. A thousand sailors were promptly arrested for mutiny.

Soldiers and sailors in Kiel held mass meetings to protest against the arrests. They feared that their comrades would be shot for mutiny. Workers joined their protests. Led by socialists, they set up a workers' and soldiers' council, or 'soviet', to run the town. Troops which came to stop this rebellion soon joined the rebels.

The mutiny leads to a revolution

The mutiny at Kiel quickly spread. Over the next week, soldiers and sailors set up soviets to run the towns where they lived. Everywhere,

Source 3 The German Socialists in 1918.

The Social Democratic Party

Leaders Friedrich Ebert
Philip Scheidemann
Membership approx 1,000,000

Aims:
1 Germany to be a Republic.
2 Germany to be governed by a national parliament elected by all Germans aged 18+.
3 Army to continue as Germany's main armed force. Authority of officers to be maintained.
4 Existing local government, law courts, police and civil service to continue to run the country.
5 Key industries and companies to be gradually nationalised.
6 People to have right of free speech, right to join trade unions etc.
7 Welfare benefits for workers, e.g. sickness and unemployment benefit, an 8 hour day, etc.

Methods
Hold elections for a national parliament. Allow the elected parliament to decide the future of Germany.

Independent Social Democratic Party

Leader Hugo Haase
Membership approx 300,000

Aims
1 Germany to be a Republic.
2 Germany to be governed by workers' and soldiers' councils elected in each town, working with a national parliament.
3 Army to be reformed: officers to be elected, badges of rank abolished, soldiers' councils to be in charge of discipline. A national militia to be created.
4 Immediate nationalisation of key industries and companies. Large estates to be broken up and sold.
5 People to have right of free speech, right to join trade unions etc.
6 Welfare benefits for workers, e.g. sickness and unemployment benefit, 8 hour day etc.

Methods
1 Strikes.
2 Trade union action in factories.
3 Co-operation with Ebert until a parliament was elected.

The Spartacus League

Leaders Rosa Luxemburg
Karl Liebknecht
Membership approx 5,000

Aims
1 Germany to be a Republic.
2 Germany to be governed by workers' and soldiers' councils in each town. No national parliament.
3 Police and army officers to be disarmed. Army to be disbanded. Local workers' militias set up to take its place.
4 Immediate nationalisation and workers' control of all mines, factories, large companies and large estates of land.
5 People to have right of free speech and all other personal freedoms.
6 Full range of welfare benefits for workers.

Methods
1 Street demonstrations and rallies.
2 Strikes.
3 Sabotage and assassination.
4 No co-operation with Ebert. No support for the proposed parliament.

police and army officers gave up their weapons and surrendered. Kaiser Wilhelm was losing control of his country.

On 9 November the Army High Command told Wilhelm that the army could no longer support him. Without an army, he could not stop the revolution. Wilhelm had no choice but to abdicate. Friedrich Ebert, leader of the largest socialist party – the Social Democratic Party – took his place as head of the government.

What kind of government for Germany?

Now that the Kaiser had gone, the socialists who had helped start the revolution began to argue among themselves. They disagreed over the question of what kind of government Germany should now have. There were three sides to the argument, as Source 3 shows. Study each one carefully and try to find the main differences between them.

Questions

1   Look at Source 1.
   a What did the cartoonist want people to think about Kaiser Wilhelm?
   b What was happening in 1918 to make many Germans dislike Kaiser Wilhelm?

2   Look at Source 2.
   a Describe exactly what you see in the picture.
   b Why was this dangerous for the German government?

3   Study Source 3, then answer these questions:
   a What aims did the three groups have in common?
   b How did their views differ on
      (i) how Germany should be governed
      (ii) the future of the army
      (iii) the German economy
      (iv) the methods of achieving their aims?
   c Were their similarities greater or less than their differences? Explain your answer.

The Spartacist rising

Of the three socialist groups shown on page 12, the Social Democratic Party was strongest after the November Revolution. This was because its leader, Friedrich Ebert, was now head of the government. He was able to use the powers of the government to make the party stronger. He ordered improvements in people's living conditions. He ended censorship and allowed free speech. He ordered a maximum eight-hour working day, help for the unemployed, and increased food supplies. All this won him the support of many workers who might instead have supported the Spartacus League. Finally, he arranged for elections to be held in January 1919 for a new national parliament.

The Spartacists oppose Ebert

The Spartacists opposed everything that Ebert did. For them, the changes that he made did not go far enough. On the last day of 1918 they renamed themselves the German Communist Party, and made plans to seize power from him.

Fear of Communism

Many Germans were alarmed when the Spartacists renamed themselves Communists. Just over a year earlier, Communists known as Bolsheviks had overthrown the government of Russia, Germany's neighbour to the east. The new Bolshevik government immediately made huge changes. For example, they took away land from landlords and gave it to poor peasants. They put all banks and factories under government control. And they carried out a campaign of terror against their opponents, killing and torturing thousands of political prisoners, and murdering the Russian royal family.

These events spread fear throughout Europe. In Germany especially, middle- and upper-class people feared that Communism would spread from Russia. So when the Spartacists became the German Communist Party and made plans to overthrow the government, it seemed as if their fears were about to come true.

The Spartacist rising

The Spartacists tried to seize power on 5 January 1919. They occupied public buildings, organised a general strike and formed a revolutionary committee. Groups of them roamed the streets, firing guns and putting up red flags, the symbol of Communism (see pages 4–5).

But the Spartacists were doomed to failure. The day before they began their rising, Ebert had created a volunteer force of 4,000 soldiers. Known as the Free Corps, they were hard men who hated Communists and liked a fight. They were well disciplined and fully equipped.

On 10 January the Free Corps attacked. They captured a newspaper building held by the Spartacists, shot several of them and beat up the rest. The next day they captured all other occupied buildings in central Berlin. Two days later they caught the Spartacist leaders, Rosa Luxemburg and Karl Liebknecht, and murdered them.

The rising thus failed.

Source 1

Spartacists fighting a street battle against the Free Corps in Berlin in 1919.

Why was the Spartacist rising so violent?

What were the issues at stake in the Spartacist rising? Why did Socialists fight Communists with such violence?

One of the main issues at stake was the general election for a new parliament, to be held in January. The Spartacists did not believe that the new parliament would make Germany truly democratic. Rosa Luxemburg, one of the Spartacist leaders, said:

Source 2

Freiheit ('Freedom'), 17 December 1918. This was the newspaper of the Independent Social Democratic Party.

> Socialism does not mean getting together in a parliament and deciding on laws. For us, socialism means the smashing of the ruling classes with all the brutality that the working class can develop.

Rosa Luxemburg believed that the new parliament would give the middle class more power than the working class. She wanted Germany to be ruled instead by the soviets – the workers' and soldiers' councils – created in the November Revolution. When her opponents said that this would be a 'dictatorship of the working class', she wrote:

Source 3

Rosa Luxemburg, *Die Nationalversammlung* (The National Assembly), 1918.

* **The capitalist class** Middle and upper-class people such as bankers, factory owners or landowners.

> The dictatorship of the working class means democracy in the socialist sense…. It means the use of all political power to…get rid of the capitalist class*…. This kind of workers' representation is a frank and blunt declaration of war against capitalism.

That view is reflected in the poster in Source 4.

Source 4

This poster says, 'Vote for Spartacus.' It shows a giant fist smashing Germany's parliament chamber, forcing members of parliament to run away.

The Spartacist rising began on 5 January, two weeks before the election for parliament was to take place. The government issued this poster, criticising Rosa Luxemburg's view of democracy:

Source 5

Quoted in Eric Waldman, *The Spartacist Rising of 1919*, 1958.

Fellow citizens!

Spartacus is now fighting for total power. The government, which...wants the people to decide their own future freely (by voting in the election) is to be overthrown by force. The people are not to be allowed to speak.... You have seen the results. Where Spartacus rules, all personal freedom and security is abolished. The newspapers are suppressed. Traffic is at a standstill. Parts of Berlin are the scene of bloody battles. Others are already without water and light. Food warehouses are being attacked. Food supplies...are being stopped. The government is taking all measures necessary to destroy this rule of terror.

Further evidence of why the government hated the Spartacists can be seen in the poster in Source 6 which it issued early in 1919 to stop people from supporting them.

Source 6

This poster was made by the government in January 1919. It shows a monster coming towards Germany from Russia. The writing says 'The Homeland is in danger' (lines 1–2). 'The tidal wave of Communism (Bolschewismus) threatens our country!' (lines 3–4).

Questions

1   Study Sources 2 and 3. Find two things that the Spartacists said they would destroy if they took power.

2   Look at Source 4. This shows a Spartacist smashing Germany's parliament. What, instead of parliament, did the Spartacists want to help govern Germany?

3   Study Sources 5 and 6. In your own words, explain how these posters tried to make people think that Communism was dangerous.

4   Using Sources 2–6 as well as the text in this section, explain why Spartacists and their opponents fought each other so violently in 1919.

The Weimar Republic

On 19 January 1919, 30 million Germans went to the polls to elect a new parliament. The most votes went to three parties which supported Ebert – the Social Democratic Party, the Centre Party and the Democrats.

The new parliament met on 6 February. Because of the fighting between Spartacists and Free Corps in Berlin, it met in a south German town called Weimar. Its first action was to elect Ebert as President of Germany Its second was to make a constitution* for Germany.

* **constitution**   A set of rules about how the country should be organised and run.

How did the constitution change Germany?

When the constitution was published in August 1919, many people praised it. What was so good about it?

First, it gave all men and women over 20 the right to vote. Few other countries allowed women to vote at that time.

Second, it used PR (proportional representation) to decide which parties got seats in parliament. This was thought to be fairer than the methods used in other countries because it gave small as well as large parties a share of the seats.

Third, the constitution gave people many human and civil rights. Germans now had the right of free speech. They could travel freely and

Source 1

How the Weimar Republic was governed.

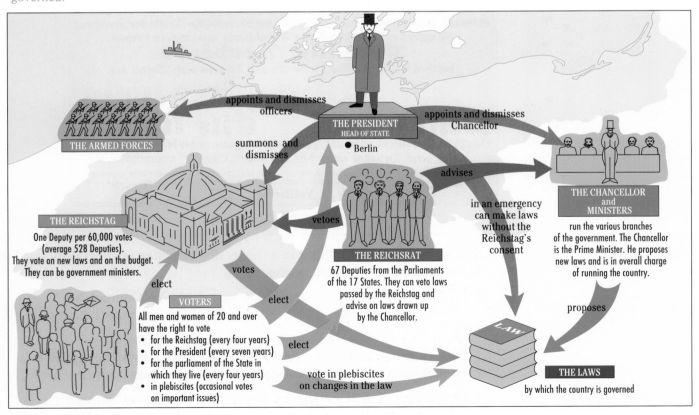

THE PRESIDENT
HEAD OF STATE
● Berlin

appoints and dismisses officers

appoints and dismisses Chancellor

summons and dismisses

advises

in an emergency can make laws without the Reichstag's consent

THE ARMED FORCES

THE CHANCELLOR and MINISTERS

run the various branches of the government. The Chancellor is the Prime Minister. He proposes new laws and is in overall charge of running the country.

vetoes

THE REICHSTAG

One Deputy per 60,000 votes (average 528 Deputies).
They vote on new laws and on the budget.
They can be government ministers.

votes

THE REICHSRAT

67 Deputies from the Parliaments of the 17 States. They can veto laws passed by the Reichstag and advise on laws drawn up by the Chancellor.

proposes

elect

VOTERS

All men and women of 20 and over have the right to vote
• for the Reichstag (every four years)
• for the President (every seven years)
• for the parliament of the State in which they live (every four years)
• in plebiscites (occasional votes on important issues)

elect

elect

vote in plebiscites on changes in the law

LAW

THE LAWS

by which the country is governed

Source 2

The Weimar Republic early in 1919 – a federation of eighteen *Länder* (states), each with an elected parliament and government to run local affairs. All the states were subject to the national government in Berlin.

hold political meetings. They had freedom of religious belief. Few other countries at that time allowed their people so many rights and freedoms.

Fourth, there were two houses of parliament. One, the Reichstag, was elected directly by all the people. The other, the Reichsrat, was made up of elected members of the eighteen German states (see Source 2). Most countries with parliaments had only one house elected by the people.

Fifth, the head of state, the President, was also elected by the people. In Britain, the head of state – a king or queen – inherited the post.

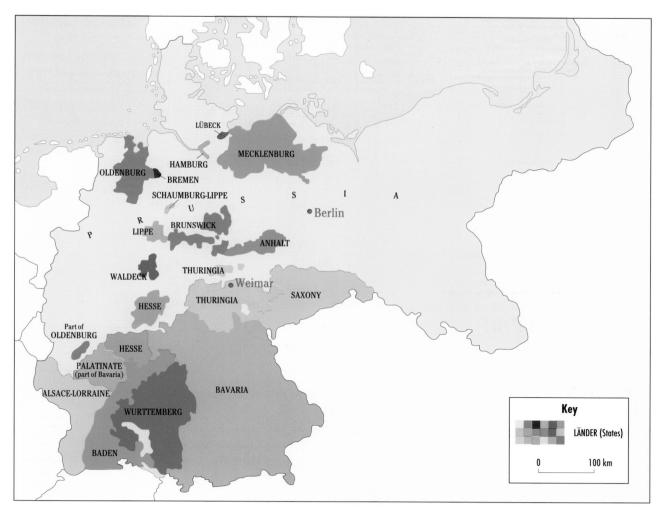

Questions

1 **a** Find Sources 1 and 2 on pages 6–7 and Sources 1 and 2 on pages 18–19.
   b Divide a page into three columns. Put these headings in column 1:
   - The head of state
   - The Reichstag (parliament)
   - The electors
   - The government
   - The method of election
   - The states
   c Show, in column 2, ways in which Germany was changed by the Weimar constitution. In column 3, show ways in which Germany was not changed by the constitution. All the information is in the sources.

2 Study columns 2 and 3. How much did the constitution change the way in which Germany was organised and governed? Explain your answer.

Unit 1 Review

Was hat uns die Revolution gebracht? — What has the Revolution brought us?

Eine Volksrepublik!
Gleiches Wahlrecht! Frauenwahlrecht!
Wahlrecht vom 20. Jahre an!
— A People's Republic!

Alle Dynastien
und ihr Hof verschwunden! Eine sozialistische Regierung!
— All royal families and their courts have vanished

Arbeiter- und Soldatenräte überall!
Das privilegierte Herrenhaus beseitigt!
Das Dreiklassen-Abgeordnetenhaus aufgelöst!
— Workers' and Soldiers' Councils everywhere!

Versammlungsfreiheit!
Koalitionsfreiheit! Pressfreiheit! Freie Religionsübung!
Aufhebung der Schulaufsicht!
— Freedom of Assembly!

Zerschmetterung des Militarismus!
Gleiche Kost für Offizier und Mann! Erhöhung der Mannschaftslöhne!
Sofortige Entlassung aller alten Leute und der Berufswichtigen!
— The destruction of militarism!

Achtstundentag!
Arbeitslosenfürsorge! Arbeitgeber und Arbeiter gleichberechtigt!
— An eight hour day!

Gemeinsame Verwaltung
der Arbeitsnachweise durch Arbeitgeber und Arbeiter!
Alle Arbeiterschutzbestimmungen wieder eingesetzt!
— Job appointments to be made by workers and employers!

Aufhebung der Gesindeordnung!
Landlieferungsverbände für Siedelungsland!
Aufhebung der Gutsbezirke!
— An end to restrictive rules for farm workers!

Erhöhung der allgemeinen Brotration!
Öffnung der Grenzen für Lebensmittel!
— An increase in the bread ration

**So viel ist schon errungen —
viel mehr muß noch erreicht werden!
Schließt die Reihen! Hütet Euch vor Zersplitterung!**
— So much has already been achieved. Much more remains to be done!

Einigkeit! — Unity!

This poster appeared in Germany in 1919. Study the translated words and then answer the questions beneath. Use the material in Unit 1 (pages 4–19) to help you answer them.

Questions

1 Explain briefly in your own words what the poster meant by:
a The Revolution (line 2)
b A People's Republic (line 3)
c All royal families and their courts have vanished (lines 6–7)
d Workers' and Soldiers' Councils (line 8)
e Freedom of assembly (lines 11–13)
f An eight-hour day (line 17).

2 The poster was boasting about good things achieved by the Revolution. But it does not say who wrote it. Which of the following do you think was most likely to have written the poster? Explain your answer.
a The Spartacus League
b The Independent Social Democratic Party
c President Ebert's government
d The Free Corps

3 The poster tells us only about good things that resulted from the Revolution. Were there any bad results of the Revolution that you think should be mentioned in order to give a balanced view of it? Explain your answer.

Unit 2 · Threats to democracy: the crises of 1919–23

The first five years of the Weimar Republic were full of difficulties. The difficulties started when the new government was forced to sign a harsh peace treaty, giving up huge amounts of land, equipment and money to the Allies. Most Germans hated the treaty. Ex-soldiers murdered hundreds of politicians who agreed to it. Extremists tried to overthrow the government. Failure to keep to the terms of the treaty led to a French invasion of Germany in 1923, and to the collapse of the German economy. All these problems threatened to kill the system of democracy created in 1919.

The 1918 Revolution did not end people's hardship. This photograph shows women, men and children, queuing for eggs, butter and cheese in Berlin in 1922.

The 'dictated peace'

The armistice

The First World War ended on 11 November 1918 when the Germans signed an armistice with the Allies. An armistice is an agreement to stop fighting while a peace treaty is drawn up.

When they signed the armistice, the Germans believed that the treaty would be based on a fourteen-point peace plan devised by President Wilson of the USA. As Wilson's Fourteen Points contained a number of fair and democratic ideas, the Germans assumed that the treaty would also be fair and democratic.

The Paris peace conference

The work of writing the treaty was done by a peace conference which began in Paris in January 1919. The Germans, however, were not allowed to take part in the conference. They were not even told anything about the talks which took place there. Lacking information, most Germans went on thinking that the treaty would be a fair one, based on the Fourteen Points.

Their hopes were shattered on 7 May 1919 when the finished treaty was put before the German government. It was much harsher than they had expected.

The terms of the treaty

Only the first part of the treaty was based on the Fourteen Points. This created a world peace-keeping organisation called the League of Nations. The rest of the treaty was designed to weaken Germany so that it could never fight another war.

As you can see from Source 1, the treaty took over 70,000 square kilometres of land from Germany and gave it to nearby countries. It also took away all Germany's colonies overseas. It slashed the size of the army and navy, and scrapped its air force. Allied armies were to occupy all parts of Germany west of the River Rhine. German forces were not allowed within 50 kilometres of the Rhine.

Finally, the treaty blamed Germany for starting the First World War and for causing all the Allies' loss and damage. It ordered Germany to pay reparations to the Allies – that is, the cost of repairing the war damage.

German reactions to the treaty

A storm of protest greeted the treaty. Mass demonstrations took place against it. Places of amusement closed down. A period of national mourning began.

The German government protested angrily but could not persuade the Allies to change the treaty. The Allies gave them five days in which to accept it. If they refused to do so, they said they would invade Germany.

Many Germans would have preferred to fight the Allies rather than sign. But the army generals warned the government that the army would be beaten if it tried to do so. Reluctantly, the German parliament voted to accept the treaty. On 28 June, two government ministers went to the Palace of Versailles, near Paris. There they signed the treaty which was then known as the Treaty of Versailles.

Source 1

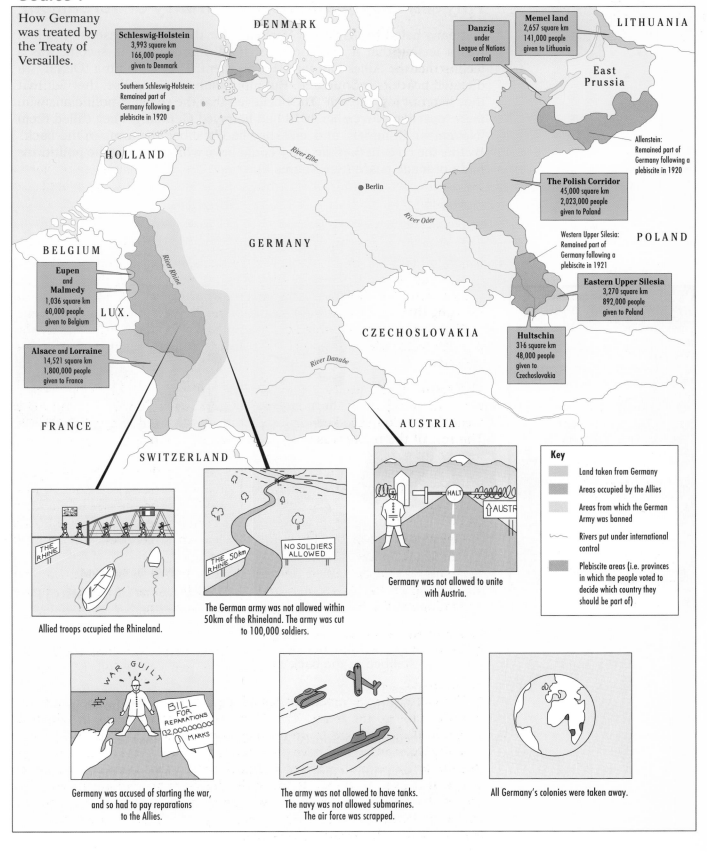

How Germany was treated by the Treaty of Versailles.

Schleswig-Holstein
3,993 square km
166,000 people
given to Denmark

Southern Schleswig-Holstein:
Remained part of
Germany following a
plebiscite in 1920

DENMARK

Memel land
2,657 square km
141,000 people
given to Lithuania

LITHUANIA

Danzig
under
League of Nations
control

East
Prussia

Allenstein:
Remained part of
Germany following a
plebiscite in 1920

The Polish Corridor
45,000 square km
2,023,000 people
given to Poland

HOLLAND

River Elbe

Berlin

River Oder

GERMANY

River Rhine

Western Upper Silesia:
Remained part of
Germany following a
plebiscite in 1921

POLAND

BELGIUM

Eupen
and
Malmedy
1,036 square km
60,000 people
given to Belgium

LUX.

Eastern Upper Silesia
3,270 square km
892,000 people
given to Poland

Alsace and **Lorraine**
14,521 square km
1,800,000 people
given to France

CZECHOSLOVAKIA

River Danube

Hultschin
316 square km
48,000 people
given to
Czechoslovakia

FRANCE

AUSTRIA

SWITZERLAND

Key

Land taken from Germany

Areas occupied by the Allies

Areas from which the German
Army was banned

Rivers put under international
control

Plebiscite areas (i.e. provinces
in which the people voted to
decide which country they
should be part of)

Germany was not allowed to unite
with Austria.

Allied troops occupied the Rhineland.

The German army was not allowed within
50km of the Rhineland. The army was cut
to 100,000 soldiers.

Germany was accused of starting the war,
and so had to pay reparations
to the Allies.

The army was not allowed to have tanks.
The navy was not allowed submarines.
The air force was scrapped.

All Germany's colonies were taken away.

Why did Germans hate the Treaty of Versailles?

Germans hated the Treaty of Versailles for three main reasons. The first was a feeling that it was too harsh (see Source 2). The second was a feeling that the Allies had forced it on them. They called it a 'Diktat' – a dictated peace (see Source 3). But more than anything else, they felt that they had not lost the war. They believed that the socialist politicians who made peace in November 1918 had betrayed Germany. They called them 'November Criminals' and said they had 'stabbed the army in the back'. By this they meant that the army could have won the war if the politicians had not made peace (See Source 4).

Source 2

This picture appeared in a German school textbook in 1933. From top to bottom, it shows losses of people, land, cattle, wheat, rye, potatoes, coal-mines, zinc, iron ore and merchant ships.

Source 3

This German cartoon shows a German signing the treaty. Five of the Allies – Italy, Britain, the USA, Japan and France – are holding guns at his head.

Source 4

This poster of 1924 asks 'Who in the World War stabbed the German army in the back...?' It accuses the Social Democratic Party of doing so.

Questions

1. Look at Source 4. Explain in your own words the idea that the German army was 'stabbed in the back'.

2. Study Sources 1 and 2.
   a Why do you think Germans so hated losing the land shown in Source 1?
   b What, according to Source 2, did Germany also lose as a result of the treaty?
   c How do you think Germany might have been affected by losing all these things?

3. Using Sources 1–4, make a short list of the complaints of German people about the Treaty of Versailles.

Risings and murders

Most Germans quickly accepted their new form of government, set up in 1919. Extremists did not. Over the next five years they carried out a series of armed risings, or putsches, against the government.

The Kapp Putsch

The first rising nearly succeeded. It took place in March 1920 when 5,000 of the Free Corps marched into Berlin (see Source 1). The government fled from the city. An extreme nationalist, Doctor Kapp, set himself up as head of a new government. His aim was to recover the land taken from Germany by the Versailles Treaty, and to rebuild Germany's military strength.

Source 1

Free Corps supporters of Doctor Kapp arrive in Berlin on an armoured train in March 1920.

Kapp was defeated by the people of Berlin. Workers in the city organised a general strike. As a result, Berlin ground to a halt. No trains or buses ran. There was no water, gas or electricity. Civil servants refused to give him money. Kapp thus had to abandon his plans. On 18 March, he and his supporters fled to Sweden and the government returned to Berlin.

Red rising in the Ruhr

No sooner had Kapp fled than workers in several parts of Germany tried to start a communist revolution. In the Ruhr industrial area they formed a 'Red Army' and took control of many towns. Desperate to restore order, the government sent Free Corps as well as regular army units into the rebel areas. Brutal fighting left a thousand workers dead.

Political murders

After using Free Corps units to crush the Red rising in the Ruhr, the government disbanded them. Some ex-members formed murder squads to carry on their fight against socialists and communists. Between 1921 and 1923 they murdered 356 people, including several leading politicians.

The troubles of 1923

1923 was a year of deep crisis. As you will see (page 30), the German economy collapsed in 1923. In the chaos that followed, socialists and communists took over Saxony and Thuringia. Workers in Hamburg seized control of working-class districts. In the Rhineland, several groups tried to break away from Germany to form independent states. In the east, troops known as the Black Reichswehr seized the town of Küstrin. And in Munich, capital of Bavaria, the National Socialist, or 'Nazi', Party tried to start a so-called 'National Revolution'.

Source 2

Political violence in Germany, 1919–23.

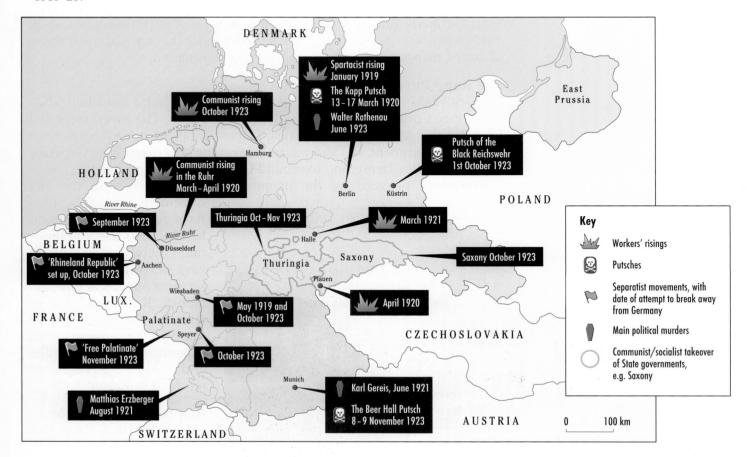

Why was there so much violence between 1919 and 1923?

One way of answering this question is to examine the motives of people who used violence against the government. First, the Free Corps. Source 3 is a recruiting poster that appeared in a newspaper in Berlin in 1919.

Source 3

Vorwärts ('Forwards'), Berlin, January 1919.

* **The Poles** Soldiers from Poland, Germany's eastern neighbour, who were trying to take land from Germany.

COMRADES

The Spartacist danger has not yet been removed.
The Poles* press ever further onto German soil.
Can you look on these things with calm?
NO!
Think what your dead comrades would say!
Soldiers, arise! Prevent Germany from becoming
the laughing stock of the world. Enrol NOW in
THE HUELSEN FREE CORPS

Source 4 is part of a letter written by a Free Corps soldier to his family:

Source 4

Maximilien Scheer, *Blut und Ehre* ('Blood and Honour'), 1937.

* **Reds** Communists.
* **Red Cross** As used here, it means the Communist Party.

> Wischerhöfen, 2 April 1920
> The enthusiasm (of the Free Corps) is terrific – unbelievable. Our battalion has had two deaths, the Reds* 200–300. Anyone who falls into our hands gets the rifle butt and then is finished off with a bullet…. We even shot ten Red Cross* nurses on sight because they were carrying pistols. We shot those little women with pleasure – how they cried and pleaded with us to spare their lives. No chance! Anyone with a gun is our enemy.

Why did the Communists use violence against the government? Source 5 suggests one answer. It is part of a letter written to a Social Democrat newspaper in 1919.

Source 5

Westfälische Allgemeine Volkszeitung ('Westphalian People's Times'), 13 March 1919.

> Our government does little to ensure the fair distribution of food…. There is bacon in the windows (of butchers' shops) but the workers cannot afford to buy it…. Every day 800 people die of starvation…and the children who die are not the children of the rich. For how long will such injustice be allowed to go on?… The time might not be too distant when a general strike will brush away this government.

In 1920, a Communist newspaper in the Ruhr industrial region stated that:

Source 6

Dortmunder General-Anzeiger ('Dortmund Reporter'), 20 March 1920.

* **red flag** The communist flag.
* **Soviets** Governing councils of workers and soldiers.

> There can only be one salvation for the German people. The red flag* must wave over the whole of Germany. Germany must become a Republic of Soviets* and, in union with Russia, the springboard for… World Revolution and World Socialism.

In Hamburg, a Russian Communist named Larissa Reisner witnessed the Communist rising of 1923. She wrote in her diary:

Source 7

Adapted from Larissa Reisner, *Hamburg at the Barricades*, 1924.

> Since August of last year Hamburg has become the arena of successive wage battles (and) for an eight-hour day…. It has also become the arena of a range of political demands: a workers' government, control of factories, and so forth….

Questions

1   Read Source 3. Find at least three ways in which the poster tried to persuade men to join the Free Corps.

2   Judging by Source 4, what kind of men joined the Free Corps?

3   Sources 5, 6 and 7 show two kinds of reason why Communists used violence against the government. One was economic – that is, to do with money and work – and the other was political – that is, to do with getting more power and a greater say in how the country was run. Using Sources 5, 6 and 7, make a short list of (a) economic reasons, and (b) political reasons why Communists used violence against the government.

Reparations and the Ruhr

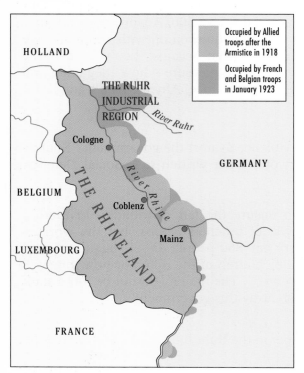

Source 1

The occupation of the Ruhr Valley and the Rhineland.

The Treaty of Versailles ordered Germany to pay 'reparations' to the Allies. This meant paying the Allies the cost of repairing the damage done to them in the First World War. The amount was 132,000 million gold marks (£6,600 million, which is about £112,000 million in today's prices).

The Germans paid the first instalment of this huge bill in 1921. In 1922, however, they announced that they could not afford any payments for the next three years. The French refused to believe this. They invaded the Ruhr industrial region to take what they were owed by force.

The invasion began on 9 January 1923. About 60,000 French and Belgian soldiers took control of every mine, factory, steelworks and railway in the region. They took food and supplies from shops. They set up machine-gun posts in the streets.

What were the consequences of the occupation of the Ruhr?

The German government could not take military action against the French because the armed forces had been so severely cut by the Treaty of Versailles. Instead it ordered the people of the Ruhr to use 'passive resistance' against them. A French army officer explained what this meant:

Source 2

Un An d'Occupation: l'Oeuvre Franco-Belge dans la Ruhr en 1923 ('A Year of Occupation: Franco-Belgian Operations in the Ruhr in 1923'). This was the official French army account of the occupation, published in 1924.

Passive resistance consisted...of not collaborating in any way with the French and Belgians. It meant refusing all their demands, and not complying with any of their orders.... The post, telegraph and telephone workers refused to make any communication with the French and Belgians, to send their letters, to sell them stamps, and so on. Railway workers refused to run the trains needed for the troops. German officials of all ranks pretended to be unaware of the presence of the French and Belgians.

The passive resistance campaign had rapid results, as Source 3 shows. It is part of a report sent to the British Foreign Office by a British embassy official in Germany.

Source 3

Foreign Office, *Memorandum of the Commercial Secretary of the British Embassy in Berlin*, 1 August 1923.

Canals and harbours are literally blocked with vessels of all types unable or unwilling to move; postal and telegraph services are seriously impeded and telephone communications cut off. Passenger railway traffic scarcely exists, motor cars have ceased to circulate.... The fuel supply and iron ore deliveries to the steel works...are cut off.... The production in the Ruhr of pig-iron and steel has sunk to about one-fifth of the pre-occupation output.

The French responded to the passive resistance campaign by expelling around 150,000 people from the region when they refused to take orders. Sometimes they used their guns on people who refused to do what they were told. During the eight months of the occupation they shot dead 132 Germans. One of those who died was a seven-year-old boy. According to the French army, he was shot accidentally by a soldier cleaning his rifle. A German nationalist newspaper told a different story:

Source 4

Deutsche Allgemeine Zeitung ('The All-German Times'), 13 June 1923.

The children were playing in a field which the invaders had declared out of bounds. When the children wouldn't leave the field, the soldier took up position, loaded his rifle before their eyes, and fired at a seven-year-old boy who was standing laughing six metres away from him. He was shot through the temples. The brave soldier then threw himself upon the corpse in order, according to one witness, to establish whether his adversary was dead, and, according to another witness, in order to eat the boy's brains.

Source 5

A French magazine cover shows French soldiers (right) in the Ruhr in January 1923. The caption says '…At the gates of every public building and factory, the blue helmets of our soldiers remind the forgetful Germans of France's rightful claims….'

Questions

1　Read Source 2.
　a Give at least three examples of German people's 'passive resistance'.
　b What do you think they hoped to achieve by doing these things?

2　Judging by Source 3, how successful was the passive resistance campaign? Explain your answer.

3　Read Source 4 carefully.
　a In your own words, briefly summarise the story.
　b It was not true that French soldiers ate their enemies' brains. Suggest why the newspaper reported such a stupid thing.
　c If you were a French reporter writing about this story for a French newspaper, which parts of the story would you report differently? How would you do so?

4　Imagine that the picture in Source 5 was for a German rather than a French magazine. How might the caption for the picture be different?

Hyperinflation

The occupation of the Ruhr led to severe problems in Germany. As the government told the Ruhr workers not to work for the French, it had to pay them for the wages they lost. Before long, the government was paying out trillions of marks each week. And because the coal-mines in the Ruhr were not producing coal, the government also had to buy huge amounts of coal from overseas.

The only way the government could raise such large sums of money was to print huge numbers of banknotes. This, however, led to inflation, which means that the value of money went down as prices went up. The more money the government printed, the faster prices went up. Prices rose so fast that 1923 became a year of hyperinflation.

How did hyperinflation affect the Germans?

Hyperinflation affected nearly everybody in Germany. It affected them by forcing up the prices of essential goods (see Source 1).

Source 1

William Guttmann and Patricia Meehan, *The Great Inflation. Germany 1919–23*, 1975.

Item	Price in marks in		
	1913	summer 1923	November 1923
1 kg loaf of bread	0.29	1,200	428,000,000,000
1 egg	0.08	5,000	80,000,000,000
1 kg of butter	2.70	26,000	6,000,000,000,000
1 kg of beef	1.75	18,800	5,600,000,000,000
1 pair of shoes	12.00	1,000,000	32,000,000,000,000

Such steep price rises caused terrible hardship for millions of people. Hardest hit were people who lived on fixed incomes such as a pension. Unlike a worker, who could ask the employer for a wage rise, a pensioner had no way of getting a rise. Source 2 shows how serious this problem was.

Source 2

Dorothy Haenkel, a German living in Frankfurt in 1923, interviewed by William Guttmann and Patricia Meehan, in *The Great Inflation, Germany 1919–23*, 1975.

A friend of mine was in charge of the office that had to deal with the giving out of...pensions...in the district around Frankfurt.... One case which came her way was the widow of a policeman who had died early, leaving four children. She had been awarded three months of her husband's salary (as a pension). My friend worked out the sum with great care...and sent the papers on as required to Wiesbaden. There they were checked, rubber stamped and sent back to Frankfurt. By the time all this was done, and the money finally paid to the widow, the amount she received would only have paid for three boxes of matches.

As Source 2 shows, hyperinflation was so rapid that money could lose its value within a day. At the peak of hyperinflation in 1923, workers were therefore paid daily rather than weekly. Even then there were problems, as Source 3 shows.

Source 3

Willy Derkow, a student in Germany in 1923, interviewed by William Guttmann and Patricia Meehan in *The Great Inflation, Germany 1919–23*, 1975.

At eleven in the morning a siren sounded. Everybody gathered in the factory yard where a five-ton lorry was drawn up, loaded with paper money. The chief cashier and his assistants climbed up on top. They read out names and just threw out bundles of notes. As soon as you caught one you made a dash for the nearest shop and bought anything that was going….

You very often bought things you did not need. But with those things you could start to barter*. You went round and exchanged a pair of shoes for a shirt, or a pair of socks for a sack of potatoes; some cutlery or crockery, for instance, for tea or coffee or butter. And this process was repeated until you eventually ended up with the thing you actually wanted.

* **barter** To swap.

By November 1923, the German mark had become worthless, as Source 4 suggests.

Source 4

This German woman was photographed in 1923 using banknotes instead of coal to heat the cooking range in her kitchen.

Questions

1 Look carefully at Sources 1–4. Make a list of ways in which German people were affected by hyperinflation.

2 Study this list of five kinds of people living in Germany in 1923:
- an ex-soldier, wounded in the First World War, now living on an army pension
- an old woman, living on her life savings which she keeps under her mattress
- a farming family, living mostly on food they grow for themselves
- a factory worker, living on wages paid daily
- a widow with three children, living on a widow's pension.

a Three of those kinds of people suffered badly from hyperinflation. Which do you think they were? Explain why they suffered so badly.

b Two of those kinds of people did not suffer as badly as the others. Which do you think they were? Explain why they did not suffer as badly as the others.

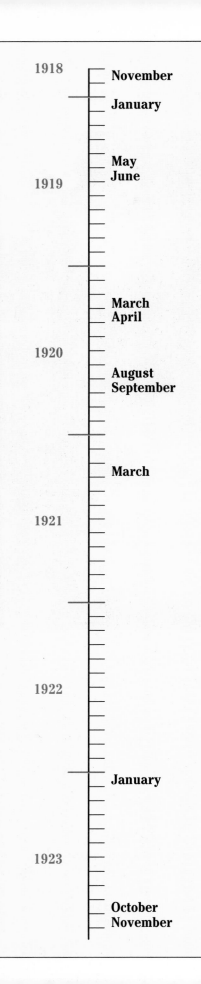

1918	November
	January
	May
1919	June
	March
	April
1920	August
	September
	March
1921	
1922	
	January
1923	
	October
	November

Unit 2 Review

1 Make a time-line like the one on the left. It should be 247 mm long, start in November 1918 and end in December 1923.

2 Add the following events to the time-line:
   a the armistice (page 22)
   b the Treaty of Versailles (page 22)
   c the French invasion of the Ruhr (page 28)
   d the German mark becomes completely worthless (page 31).

3 Now look at Source 2 on page 26. Add to the time-line:
   a workers' risings
   b putsches
   c takeovers of state governments

4 Look at your completed time-line. In which two of the years 1918–23 was the new German government in greatest danger of being overthrown?

5 What was the main cause of the unrest in each of those two years?

6 If the first of those causes had not existed, would any of the unrest between 1919 and 1923 have taken place? Explain your answer.

Unit 3 · Enemies of democracy: Hitler and the Nazis

One of the many groups that hated the Weimar Republic was the National Socialist German Workers' Party – Nazi Party for short. Founded in 1919 with 50 members, it soon became Germany's fastest growing party. In 1923 its leader, Adolf Hitler, tried to overthrow the government. He failed, and was sent to prison. But this did not kill the party. In his prison cell, Hitler plotted new tactics for overthrowing the Weimar Republic. These tactics would succeed in destroying it less than ten years later.

This unit takes a close look at the Nazis. It asks three questions: what kind of person was their leader, Adolf Hitler; what kind of people became Nazis; and why did they want to destroy the Weimar Republic?

Nazi Stormtroopers taking part in a demonstration in Munich on 1 May 1923.

What sort of person was Hitler?

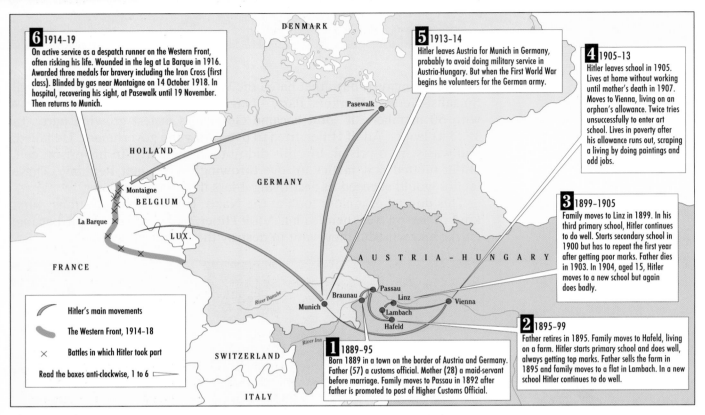

6 1914–19
On active service as a despatch runner on the Western Front, often risking his life. Wounded in the leg at La Barque in 1916. Awarded three medals for bravery including the Iron Cross (first class). Blinded by gas near Montaigne on 14 October 1918. In hospital, recovering his sight, at Pasewalk until 19 November. Then returns to Munich.

5 1913–14
Hitler leaves Austria for Munich in Germany, probably to avoid doing military service in Austria-Hungary. But when the First World War begins he volunteers for the German army.

4 1905–13
Hitler leaves school in 1905. Lives at home without working until mother's death in 1907. Moves to Vienna, living on an orphan's allowance. Twice tries unsuccessfully to enter art school. Lives in poverty after his allowance runs out, scraping a living by doing paintings and odd jobs.

3 1899–1905
Family moves to Linz in 1899. In his third primary school, Hitler continues to do well. Starts secondary school in 1900 but has to repeat the first year after getting poor marks. Father dies in 1903. In 1904, aged 15, Hitler moves to a new school but again does badly.

2 1895–99
Father retires in 1895. Family moves to Hafeld, living on a farm. Hitler starts primary school and does well, always getting top marks. Father sells the farm in 1895 and family moves to a flat in Lambach. In a new school Hitler continues to do well.

1 1889–95
Born 1889 in a town on the border of Austria and Germany. Father (57) a customs official. Mother (28) a maid-servant before marriage. Family moves to Passau in 1892 after father is promoted to post of Higher Customs Official.

Legend:
- Hitler's main movements
- The Western Front, 1914–18
- × Battles in which Hitler took part
- Read the boxes anti-clockwise, 1 to 6

Source 1
Hitler's first thirty years, 1889–1919.

You can see from Source 1 that Hitler was not German. He was born in Austria-Hungary, and lived there until he was 24. Only then did he go to live in Germany. What sort of person was he? Make up your own mind after studying Sources 1–5.

Source 2
Hitler's final school report, dated September 1905. Quoted in Konrad Heiden, *Der Fuehrer. Hitler's Rise to Power*, 1944.

* **moral conduct** Behaviour.
* **diligence** Care and thoroughness.
* **inadequate** Not good enough.
* **laudable** Deserves praise.
* **stenography** Shorthand writing.

	First session	Second session
Moral conduct*	satisfactory	satisfactory
Diligence*	unequal	inadequate*
Religion	adequate	satisfactory
German language	inadequate	adequate
Geography and history	adequate	satisfactory
Mathematics	inadequate	satisfactory
Chemistry	adequate	adequate
Physics	satisfactory	adequate
Geometry and technical drawing	adequate	inadequate† adequate#
Freehand drawing	laudable*	excellent
Gymnastics	excellent	excellent
Stenography*	inadequate	—
Singing	—	satisfactory
External form of written work	displeasing	displeasing

† Repeat examination permitted   # After repeating the examination

Source 3

One of Hitler's teachers recalling in 1923 what he was like as a pupil. Quoted by August Kubizek, Hitler's closest childhood friend, in *The Young Hitler I Knew*, 1954.

Hitler was certainly gifted, although only for particular subjects, but he lacked self-control and, to say the least, he was considered argumentative, autocratic*, self-opinionated* and bad-tempered, and unable to submit to school discipline. Nor was he industrious, otherwise he would have achieved much better results, gifted as he was.

* **autocratic** Bossy.
* **self-opinionated** Unable to accept other people's views.

Source 4

From a letter written by Hitler to an admirer who had asked him for information about himself. Quoted in Werner Masur, *Hitler's Letters and Notes*, 1973.

* **anti-semite** Someone who hates Jewish people.

I was born on 20 April 1889, in Braunau am Inn, the son of a local post official Alois Hitler. My entire schooling consisted of five years at Primary School and four years of Middle School....I was orphaned at the age of 17 years and...was forced to earn my living as a simple worker. I became a labourer on a building site and during the next two years did every conceivable type of casual labour.... The school of harsh reality turned me into an anti-semite* within barely a year.

With tremendous effort I was able to teach myself to paint in my spare time and this so well that from the age of 20 I earned ... a bare livelihood by this work.... I became an architectural draughtsman and painter and by the age of 21 I was almost completely independent.

Source 5

A letter written by Hitler's commanding officer in 1918, quoted in G.Ward Price, *I Know These Dictators*, 1937.

* **engagements** Battles.
* **company-runner**
A messenger who carries messages from one commander to another during a battle.

Lance-Corporal (Volunteer) Hitler, Third Company

Hitler has been with the regiment since the beginning of the war, and has given a splendid account of himself in all the engagements* in which he has taken part.

As company-runner* he displayed, both in open and trench warfare, exemplary coolness and spirit, and he was always ready to carry through messages in the most difficult positions and at great risk to his life....

Hitler received the Iron Cross (second class) for gallant conduct in the Battle of Wytschaete on 2 December 1914. I regard him as fully worthy to be decorated with the Iron Cross (first class).

Questions

1   In groups, find out all you can from Sources 1–5 about Hitler's
   a family background
   b school life and achievements
   c life between leaving school and joining the army
   d life as a soldier in the First World War.

2   Using Sources 2–5 only, choose six words from this list which you think describe the kind of person that Hitler was: sociable, brave, cowardly, lazy, hard-working, artistic, independent, clever, tolerant, active, intolerant. For each word you choose, explain why you think it is an accurate description of his character.

Origins and growth of the Nazi Party

Hitler stayed in the army at the end of the war. Early in 1919 he was sent to Munich, the capital of Bavaria, to keep a watch on extremist political groups to find out whether they were a danger to the government.

One of the groups which Hitler watched was called the German Workers' Party. Although he thought that it was small and poorly organised, he liked its ideas and decided to join. Soon he was one of the party's leaders. He organised meetings, put advertisements in newspapers, and stuck posters on walls. In February 1920 he changed the party's name to National Socialist German Workers' Party, and issued a 25-point programme describing its aims. An eye-catching symbol, the swastika (see Source 1) became the party's emblem.

The Nazi* Party, as it was nicknamed, grew rapidly. Its membership rose from around 50 in January 1919 to 3,000 in 1920, 6,000 in 1921, and over 50,000 in 1923. It published its own newspaper to spread Nazi views. And it created an armed force of Stormtroopers (*Sturmabteilung*, or SA) to fight its opponents.

* **Nazi**　An abbreviation of the party's German name – 'Nationalsozialistische Deutsche Arbeiterpartei'.

Source 1

A public meeting organised by the Nazi Party in a beer hall in Munich in 1923. The walls are decorated with the party's swastika emblem.

Who joined the Nazi Party, and why?

What was the attraction of the Nazi Party? Why did it grow so quickly?

One reason for its success was Hitler's ability to put across the ideas of the party to public meetings. These were often held in beer halls where large audiences could listen in comfort to speeches (see Source 1).

So what were the ideas of the Nazi Party? What were Hitler's aims? A pro-Nazi German newspaper summarised them in an article in 1922:

Source 2

Kreuzzeitung, 28 December 1922.

* **St Germain** The second of the Paris Peace Treaties of 1919. It dealt with Germany's ally, Austria-Hungary.

Hitler is in close contact with the Germans of Czechoslovakia and Austria, and he demands the union of all Germans in a greater Germany....

Hitler demands the cancellation of the Treaties of Versailles and Saint Germain* and the restoration of the German colonies.

A very important part of the Party Programme is the idea of race.... He wants only people of German race to be citizens of Germany.... He wants all immigrants into Germany since 1914 to be expelled.

Hitler opposes the parliamentary system. Hitler's party wants first of all to set up a dictatorship which will last until Germany's present troubles are ended.... The dictator in question is evidently Hitler.

The party's economic programme is as follows: ...profit-sharing among workers of profits from large companies, public ownership of big shops, help for small industry and the middle class.

Source 3

Michael H. Kater, *The Nazi Party: a Social Profile of Members and Leaders, 1919–1945*, 1983.

Who was attracted by such ideas? Some answers can be found in the party's membership records. These listed members according to their social class and by the work that they did. Source 3 is a summary of the records.

Class	Occupation	% of total
Lower class	Unskilled workers (e.g. farm workers, labourers, miners, servants)	11.9
	Skilled workers (e.g. wage-earning bakers, plumbers, electricians)	14.3
	Other skilled workers	9.7
Middle class	Master craftsmen (e.g. self-employed smiths, watchmakers, tailors)	8.3
	Lower employees (e.g. sales people, clerks, foremen)	11.8
	Lower civil servants (e.g postal workers, customs officers)	6.6
	Merchants (e.g. car dealers, wholesalers, inn-keepers)	14.4
	Farmers (e.g. farm-owners, wine makers, fishermen)	11.0
Upper middle class and aristocracy	Managers (e.g. company executives)	1.9
	Higher civil servants (e.g. tax officers, professors)	0.4
	Professionals with academic qualifications (e.g. doctors, lawyers)	2.5
	Students (e.g. senior school pupils and university students)	4.4
	Entrepreneurs (e.g. factory owners, company directors)	2.7

Questions

1 Study Source 2 which mentions nine ideas of Hitler and the Nazi Party. Make a list of them, numbered 1–9.

2 Divide a page into columns. Put these descriptions at the top:
   • a nationalist who wanted Germany to be powerful
   • a socialist who wanted the country's wealth to be shared by everyone
   • an ex-soldier who hated the Paris peace treaties
   • a nationalist who disliked non-Germans living in Germany
   • a businessman whose company was badly affected by inflation.

3 Under each heading, put the numbers of any ideas you think would have appealed to this kind of person.

4 What does your completed table tell you about the kinds of people who supported the Nazi Party in the early 1920s? Explain your answer.

The Munich Beer Hall Putsch

Source 1

Nazi Stormtroopers arrive in Munich in November 1923 to take part in the 'Beer Hall Putsch'.

The Nazi Party grew rapidly under Hitler's leadership. By late 1923 it had 55,000 members and Hitler was one of Bavaria's best-known politicians. In November he decided that the Nazis were strong enough to attempt a putsch in Munich, the Bavarian capital.

The putsch failed. Sixteen Nazis were shot dead. Hitler was arrested and sent to prison. The party was banned. With hindsight, we can now see that Hitler had made a bad mistake. What led him to think a putsch could succeed?

Why did Hitler attempt a putsch in 1923?

As you have read, Germany was in a crisis in 1923 because the French had occupied the Ruhr. The people of the Ruhr used passive resistance against them, leading to mass unemployment and to hyperinflation.

Faced with ruin, the government ended the passive resistance campaign in September. But this was an unpopular move. Many Germans wanted to continue the campaign. In Bavaria, groups called 'patriotic bands' joined together to form a 'German Fighting Union'. Led by Hitler, its aim was to overthrow the national government in Berlin. This police report described the mood of many Bavarians:

Source 2

A Bavarian police report, written in September 1923.

As a result of rising prices and increasing unemployment, the workers are bitter. The patriotic bands are at fever pitch because of the… abandonment of the Ruhr resistance….

Three weeks later, a report by the Munich city council stated that:

Source 3

Quoted in Harold J. Gordon, *Hitler and the Beer Hall Putsch*, 1972.

In all of Munich (including the food market) absolutely no potatoes have been available for days which, in view of the fact that potatoes are naturally the cheapest food, is particularly tragic at this time.

In this tense situation, Hitler planned to seize power by marching to Berlin with 15,000 men. He was opposed, however, by the Bavarian leader, Ritter von Kahr, who had his own plans. Kahr wanted to break away from Germany and make Bavaria an independent country. He tried to persuade Hitler to join forces with him, instead of marching to Berlin. But Hitler could not afford to change his plans. The leader of the Munich Stormtroopers later explained why:

Source 4

Wilhelm Brückner, leader of the Munich SA, speaking as a witness at Hitler's trial in 1924, after the putsch had failed.

> The...officers were dissatisfied because the march on Berlin was being held up. They were saying 'Hitler is a fraud just like the rest of them. You are not attacking....' And I myself said to Hitler, 'The day is coming when I will not be able to hold the men back. Unless something happens now the men will sneak away.' We had many unemployed men among us, men who had sacrificed their last pair of shoes, their last clothes, their last ten pence on training, and who thought 'Soon things will get under way and we'll be...out of this mess'.

Hitler decided not to join Kahr but he still needed Kahr's support. An opportunity to get it occurred on 8 November. On that day, Kahr held a public meeting in a large beer hall in Munich. Six hundred Stormtroopers surrounded the hall while Hitler burst in and announced that a 'national revolution' had begun. He held a gun at Kahr's head and forced him to tell the audience that he would support the revolution. Then General Ludendorff, a well-known war hero who was in on the plot, entered the hall and announced that he too supported Hitler.

These promises of support from Kahr and Ludendorff convinced the audience that Hitler was serious. Then Hitler announced:

Source 5

Quoted in John Dornberg, *The Putsch That Failed*, 1982.

* **deposed** Overthrown, no longer in power.

> I declare the government of the November Criminals in Berlin deposed*.... A new national government will be named today, right here in Bavaria, in Munich. A national German army will be established immediately. I propose that I take over the political leadership of the... government until we have settled scores with the criminals who are bringing Germany to ruin.

The next day, however, Kahr went back on his promise to support Hitler. Despite this, Hitler went ahead with his plans to march through the city with 2,000 Stormtroopers. He hoped to win public support by doing so. But as they neared the city on the morning of 9 November, armed police blocked their way, and a gun battle started between them. Sixteen Nazis were shot dead and hundreds, including Hitler, were injured.

The putsch thus failed. Hitler and Ludendorff were arrested later in the day, taken to prison, and charged with high treason.

Questions

1. Read Sources 2 and 3. Find at least four reasons why people in Bavaria were likely to support Hitler's attempt to overthrow the government.

2. Read Source 4. What might have happened to Hitler if he had *not* attempted to overthrow the government?

3. **a** In Source 5, what did Hitler mean by 'November Criminals'?
   b What does this tell you about why Hitler wanted to overthrow the government?

Trial, prison and release

Source 1

Hitler in prison with fellow Nazis in 1924.

After the Beer Hall Putsch, the Nazi Party was banned and its leaders arrested. Hitler was put on trial.

This might have been the end of Hitler's career. However, the trial received huge publicity. For the 24 days that it lasted, it was front-page news in every national newspaper. This meant that millions of people could read everything that Hitler said in his defence. As a result, Hitler's fame spread to parts of Germany where he was not well known. Support for the Nazis therefore continued to grow.

Hitler was found guilty of high treason and sentenced to five years of 'fortress detention'. This was a punishment reserved for political prisoners. With good behaviour, he would be eligible for early release after six months.

Did prison change Hitler?

Hitler began his sentence on 1 April 1924 in Landsberg fortress, not far from Munich. You can see from Source 1 that conditions in the fortress were not hard. He had a furnished room rather than a cell. He wore his own clothes. He was allowed visitors and mail every day.

Hitler spent much of his time in prison writing a book. Its title was *Mein Kampf* ('My Struggle'). It was part autobiography, part an account of his ideas. These ideas were about history, politics, race, and the future of Germany. He also spent time thinking about the future of the Nazi Party and about how to gain power. He revealed his thoughts to a visitor called Kurt Ludecke:

Source 2

Kurt Ludecke, *I Knew Hitler*, 1938.

* **armed coup** An armed rebellion against a government. Means the same as putsch.
* **enter the Reichstag** To become members of parliament by standing for election.

'From now on', he (Hitler) said, 'we must follow a new line of action.... When I resume active work it will be necessary to pursue a new policy. Instead of working to achieve power by an armed coup*, we shall have to hold our noses and enter the Reichstag*.

In order to 'resume active work', Hitler of course needed to be free. He applied for early release in September 1924, when the fortress governor wrote this report:

Source 3

Otto Lurker, *Hitler hinter Festungsmauern* ('Hitler Behind Prison Bars'), 1933.

Hitler has shown himself to be an orderly, disciplined prisoner.... He makes no exceptional demands, is calm and sensible, serious, in no way aggressive.... He is without personal vanity, is content with the prison diet, neither smokes nor drinks.... Hitler will undoubtedly try to revive enthusiasm for the National Movement as he sees it; he will not, however, employ his previous violent methods…. I have no hesitation in saying that Hitler's general behaviour under detention merits the grant of a probationary period*.

* **probationary period**
Release from prison on condition that he continued to behave well.

When the Bavarian police heard that Hitler had applied for early release, they drew up their own report on him:

Source 4

Hans Kallenbach, *Mit Adolf Hitler auf Festung Landsberg* ('With Hitler in Landsberg Fortress'), 1933.

This Headquarters urges that Hitler…should not be released….
    Many acts of violence by his followers, culminating in his putsch, are due entirely to his influence. With his energy he will without doubt encourage fresh public disturbances. He will be a permanent danger to the security of the state the moment he has been released…. Hitler will resume his ruthless struggle against the government and will not be afraid to break the law.

Despite this warning from the police, Hitler was freed from prison in December 1924. In return for a promise not to break any laws, the authorities gave him permission to re-found the banned Nazi Party. This he did in February 1925 (see Source 5).

Source 5

Hitler re-founding the Nazi Party in February 1925, following his release from prison three months earlier.

Questions

1   Read the third sentence in Source 2. In it, Hitler was saying that he would change his methods of trying to take over the government. In your own words, describe:
    a the methods he had used before going to prison
    b the new method he intended to use after release from prison.

2   Source 3 suggests that Hitler changed as a result of being in prison. In what way?

3   **a** What does Source 4 say about Hitler that is different from Source 3?
    b How might this difference be explained?

Unit 3 Review

Source 1

Nazis campaigning in a general election for the Reichstag in
December 1924. They campaigned jointly with another
party in order to get round the ban on the Nazi Party.

Review your understanding of Unit 3 by answering the questions below.

Questions

1   Identify the symbol on the flag in the photograph above.

2   To which Nazi organisation did the men on the lorry belong?

3   Judging by what you have read in Unit 3, what ideas do you think these
    Nazis were trying to put across to the public?

4   Compare the photograph on this page with the photograph on page 33.
    a How do these photographs suggest that the Nazis started using more
    democratic ways of gaining power in 1924?
    b In what ways do the Nazis in the photograph above seem *not* to have
    changed since 1923?

5   What events in the previous thirteen months led to the Nazi Party
    changing its methods of trying to gain power?

Unit 4 · The collapse of democracy: the Weimar Republic, 1924–33

Between 1924 and 1929 Germany recovered from the crisis of 1923. Germans called these years the 'Golden Twenties'. In 1929, however, an economic slump put an end to the recovery. The Golden Twenties gave way to mass unemployment, poverty and hunger in the thirties.

Many Germans blamed the government for this. In elections, they voted for extremist politicians who claimed they knew how to overcome these problems. One of them was Adolf Hitler. Between 1929 and 1933 his Nazi Party grew from being one of the smallest parties in Germany to the largest, allowing him to take power in 1933.

Unit 4 describes those events, and asks you to think about this question. How was it possible for a man who was in prison in 1924, and who led one of Germany's smallest parties, to become leader of the country less than ten years later?

An election poster shows a Nazi, a Communist and an old Free Corps soldier (right) as armed bullies. It says, 'These are the enemies of democracy! Away with them! Vote for the Social Democratic Party.'

The 'Golden Twenties', 1924–29

How did Germany recover from the 1923 crisis?

As you have read (see pages 28–31), Germany went through a terrible crisis in 1923 when the French army occupied the Ruhr. The people of the Ruhr went on strike and used 'passive resistance' against them. This led to mass unemployment and to hyperinflation.

A new government

With Germany nearing collapse, a new government was set up to overcome the crisis. First, it called off the passive resistance campaign against the French in the Ruhr. Then it replaced the worthless mark with a new currency, the *Rentenmark*. As a result of these two measures, the French agreed to leave the Ruhr, and hyperinflation stopped.

This was bad for extremists such as the Nazis, and good for moderate parties. As Germany recovered from the crisis, many people supported what the government was doing and stopped voting for the extremists.

The Dawes Plan

Germany continued to recover in 1924. This was due largely to Gustav Stresemann, Germany's Foreign Minister. Stresemann's first achievement was to persuade the French, British and Americans to accept lower reparations payments. By the Dawes Plan of 1924, Germany agreed to pay as much as it could afford each year, starting with 1,000 million marks. The USA gave Germany a loan of 800 million marks to get the plan started.

Source 1

'Risen from the mire'. A 1924 election poster for the German National People's Party shows Germany heading for a better future after being pulled clear of the problems of 1918–24.

Improving foreign relations

Stresemann's next achievement was to improve Germany's standing in the eyes of other countries. This he did by signing the Locarno Treaties in 1925 (see Source 2). By these treaties, the Germans promised never to attack France and Belgium, and to settle peacefully any disputes that might arise with countries to the east.

Germany's reputation improved further in 1926 when it was allowed to join the League of Nations. And in 1929 a new reparations plan, the Young Plan, reduced Germany's bill still further.

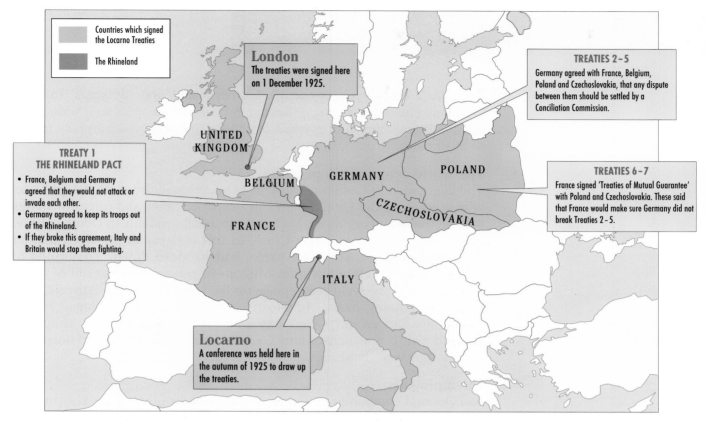

London
The treaties were signed here on 1 December 1925.

TREATIES 2–5
Germany agreed with France, Belgium, Poland and Czechoslovakia, that any dispute between them should be settled by a Conciliation Commission.

**TREATY 1
THE RHINELAND PACT**
• France, Belgium and Germany agreed that they would not attack or invade each other.
• Germany agreed to keep its troops out of the Rhineland.
• If they broke this agreement, Italy and Britain would stop them fighting.

TREATIES 6–7
France signed 'Treaties of Mutual Guarantee' with Poland and Czechoslovakia. These said that France would make sure Germany did not break Treaties 2–5.

Locarno
A conference was held here in the autumn of 1925 to draw up the treaties.

Countries which signed the Locarno Treaties

The Rhineland

UNITED KINGDOM
BELGIUM
GERMANY
POLAND
CZECHOSLOVAKIA
FRANCE
ITALY

Source 2

The Locarno Treaties of 1925.

Economic prosperity

Now that Germany no longer suffered from inflation, foreign banks were willing to lend money to German businesses and to the government. Between 1924 and 1929 foreign banks, mostly American, lent some 25,000 million gold marks to German borrowers. With this money they built nearly three million new homes. In nearly every town, new factories and public facilities sprang up. New roads and railways were built. New airships, ocean liners, radio stations, film studios and telephone networks made Germany seem the most modern and prosperous country outside the USA.

Questions

1   Look at Source 1.
   a The artist portrayed the year 1918 as a time of darkness and suffering. What events of 1918 might the artist have had in mind?
   b Give examples of events between 1918 and 1924 which also involved suffering.
   c What happened in 1923-24 to improve the situation in Germany?

2   **a** Study Source 2 and list the countries which signed the Locarno Treaties.
   b Describe the advantages of the Rhineland Pact to (i) France and Belgium, (ii) Germany.
   c Stresemann said that the Locarno Treaties were 'the beginning of a new era'. Why do you think he considered the treaties so important?

The Great Depression

Germany's recovery from the 1923 crisis lasted only six years. In 1929 Germany entered a deep economic depression. A depression is a slump in economic activities such as trade, leading to unemployment and the failure of businesses.

The world economic depression

The depression in Germany was part of a worldwide economic depression which began in the United States. It deepened when the prices of shares sold on the New York Stock Exchange dropped suddenly in October 1929. As a result of the Wall Street Crash, as this collapse of the stock market was known, many American banks had to close down. Thousands of companies went out of business. Millions of people were put out of work.

Although these events took place on the other side of the Atlantic, they affected Germany badly. American banks demanded repayment of the loans they had given to Germany since 1924 (see page 45). They also stopped giving new loans. Many German companies which had borrowed money thus went bankrupt.

Unemployment

As bankrupt companies closed down, workers lost their jobs. The number of registered unemployed rose to more than six million by early 1932 (see Source 1). In addition, there were between one and three million jobless people who could not or did not register as unemployed. Altogether, between seven and nine million Germans were out of work by 1932. Taking into account their families, who depended on their earnings, around 23 million people were directly affected by unemployment.

The Depression affected even those who were still in work. Apart from the dread of losing their jobs, millions of German workers had to put up with low wages, short-time working and worsening conditions of work.

Source 1

Unemployment in Germany, 1925–33. Figures taken from *The International Labour Review*, International Labour Office, Geneva, 1926–33.

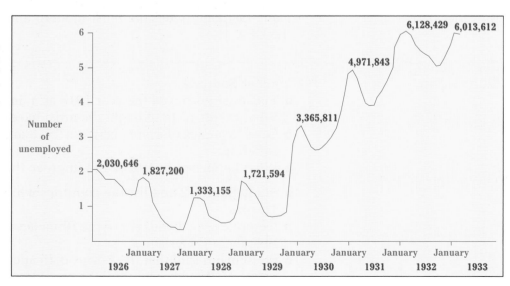

Source 2
An unemployed German looking for work in 1930. Her placard says, 'I am a trained shorthand typist, out of work, looking for any kind of work.'

Source 2
An unemployed German looking for work in 1930. Her placard says, 'I am a trained shorthand typist, out of work, looking for any kind of work.'

How did unemployment affect people's lives?

After losing their jobs, German workers were paid unemployment benefit by the government for 26 weeks. After that, they had to live on 'crisis payments' from the government. Source 3, written by a 13-year-old girl, explains the system:

Source 3

Part of an autobiography written by 'Margot L.' in December 1932, in Ruth Weiland, *Die Kinder der Arbeitslosen* ('Children of the Unemployed'), 1933.

First my father went to sign on for the dole. Later, when the time during which he could sign on ran out, he got 'crisis benefit'. He had to collect the money from the welfare. This was not enough to manage on. I often saw how my mother brooded over the question of clothing and feeding our family of six.

Source 4 gives an idea of how unemployed parents managed to feed their families. It is a diet sheet, kept by an unemployed family in the Austrian town of Marienthal, for a week in 1930. The family completed the sheet as part of a survey on unemployment carried out by researchers from Vienna University.

Source 4

	Breakfast	Lunch	Evening meal
Monday	coffee, bread	pea soup, *griessschmarrn**	coffee, bread with lard
Tuesday	coffee, bread	cabbage, potatoes	cabbage
Wednesday	coffee, bread	potato soup, *krautfleckerln**	coffee, bread
Thursday	coffee, bread	potato goulash	potato goulash
Friday	coffee, bread	soup, potato noodles	coffee, bread
Saturday	coffee, bread	potato soup, beans	coffee, bread
Sunday	coffee, white bread	soup, sweet noodles	coffee, white bread

* **griessschmarrn** Semolina pancakes.   * **krautfleckerln** Fried noodles with spiced cabbage.

Marie Jahoda, Paul L. Lazarsfeld, Hans Zeisel, *Die Arbeitslosen von Marienthal* ('The Unemployed of Marienthal'), 1933.

Many of the jobless could not afford to pay rent and thus became homeless. In Berlin, thousands of homeless families camped in woods just outside the city:

Source 5

Walther Kiaulehn, *Schicksal einer Weltstadt* ('The Fate of a Metropolis'), 1958.

Only the father went into town to collect his dole money. The more unemployed there were, the bigger the camps grew. Visitors were amazed at their quietness. You saw men sitting in front of their tents just staring out over the water. The rows of tents were neatly laid out, with street names and house numbers, and the space between the tents was decorated with patterns of slate. [But] there was nothing romantic about camp life – it was a clean, adult and neat misery.

Questions

1   Look carefully at Source 1.
     a In which year did the number of unemployed rise most quickly?
     b What was the reason for this?
     c In which year was there most unemployment?

2   a What nutrients are lacking from the family's diet in Source 4?
     b How might this diet have affected the health of the family?
     c How might living for years on this diet have affected the way the family felt about (i) themselves, (ii) the government?

The Nazis and the Depression, 1929–32

Sadly, the German government did little to help people who were out of work, hungry or homeless. It was handicapped by Germany's voting system – PR (proportional representation). This gave small as well as large parties a share of the seats in the Reichstag (parliament). As a result, there were so many parties in the Reichstag that no party ever had more than half the seats (see Source 1). This meant that no single party could ever form a government. The largest party had to join together with smaller parties to make a coalition government.

When the Depression began there were five parties in the coalition government. These parties disagreed almost every time they had to make a decision. In particular, they could not agree on how much unemployment pay the jobless should be given. One, the Social Democratic Party, wanted to increase it. Another wanted to cut it. Rather than agree to a cut, the Social Democrats resigned from the government. This meant that the government could no longer function.

Government by decree

The solution to this problem lay in Article 48 of the constitution. This allowed the President, in an emergency, to make laws without consulting the Reichstag. This was known as government by decree.

The President, General von Hindenburg, asked the leader of the medium-sized Centre Party, Heinrich Brüning, to form a new government without the Social Democrats. He intended to make Brüning's decisions into law by issuing decrees, if the Reichstag would not vote for them.

Source 1

A plan of the Reichstag showing the number of seats held by each party after the election of 1928.

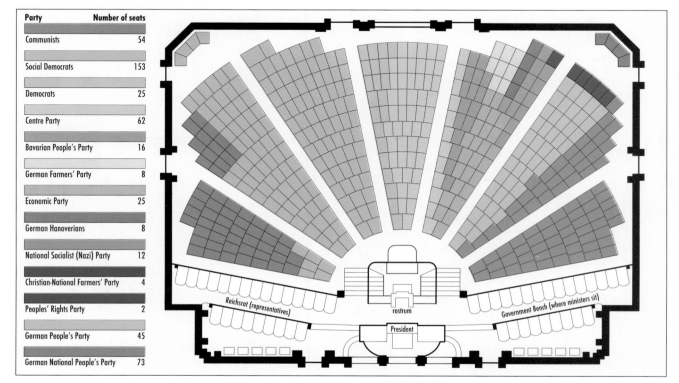

Party	Number of seats
Communists	54
Social Democrats	153
Democrats	25
Centre Party	62
Bavarian People's Party	16
German Farmers' Party	8
Economic Party	25
German Hanoverians	8
National Socialist (Nazi) Party	12
Christian-National Farmers' Party	4
Peoples' Rights Party	2
German People's Party	45
German National People's Party	73

Reichsrat (representatives)   rostrum   Government Bench (where ministers sit)

President

Helped by Hindenburg, Brüning tried to overcome the Depression by cutting government spending, cutting the wages of government workers and increasing taxes. Such measures were, of course, unpopular. When the Reichstag tried to stop them, Hindenburg simply dismissed it and ordered elections for a new Reichstag.

The elections of 1930

The elections took place in September 1930. They were a disaster for German democracy, for the Nazis increased their number of seats from twelve to 107. The Communists got 54 seats. The largest of the parties which supported democracy, the Social Democrats, lost ten seats.

Nazi propaganda

Success in these elections made the Nazis ambitious. Over the next two years they made huge efforts to increase their support further, doubling their vote in 1932. In particular, they spent huge sums of money using propaganda to win support.

Nazi ideas were spread by posters (see Source 2), by eight Nazi-owned newspapers, and by millions of pamphlets. Above all, the Nazis used mass rallies, or public meetings, to put across their message. Source 3 describes a Nazi mass rally in Berlin in July 1932, shortly before a general election.

Source 2

Passers-by stop to look at a Nazi poster that has just been put up on an advertising pillar in 1932. The poster (inset) says 'Our last hope – HITLER'.

Source 3

Kurt Ludecke, *I Knew Hitler*, 1938.

More than a hundred thousand people had paid to squeeze inside …. At home millions were waiting by the radio….

Inside the stadium, the stage-setting was flawless. Around the vast stone arena, banners were silhouetted against the darkening sky…. Directly opposite reared a dramatic speaking stand…hung with giant swastikas…. Twelve huge SA bands played military marches with beautiful precision and terrifying power….

Suddenly a wave surged over the crowd. It leaned forward. The word went round, 'Hitler is coming! Hitler is coming!' A blare of trumpets rent the air and a hundred thousand people leapt to their feet…. Then the crowd burst into a tremendous ovation, the '*Heils*'* swelling until they were like the roar of a mighty cataract.

* **heil** German for 'hail' – a form of greeting.

Source 4

Votes cast for the main parties in elections for the Reichstag, 1924–32.

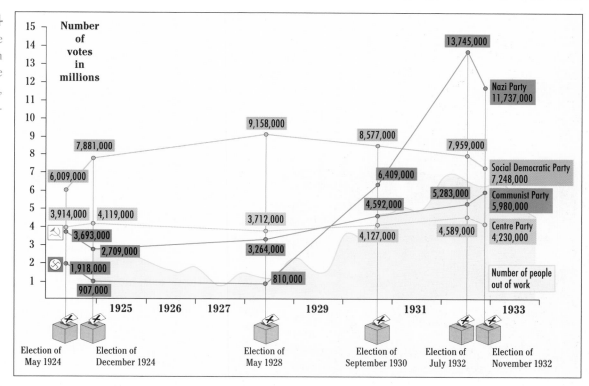

Questions

1 Look carefully at Source 1.
   a What was the total number of seats held by parties in the Reichstag?
   b Which party had most seats in the Reichstag at this time?
   c Why could that party not form a government?
   d How many extra seats would it need to form a government?
   e Which parties could it invite to share in the government, in order to get enough seats?
   f What problems might be caused by doing so?

2 Study Source 4.
   a Describe the changes in the numbers of (i) Nazi voters, (ii) Communist voters, (iii) Social Democratic voters, (iv) Centre Party voters.
   b Using Sources 2, 3 and 4, suggest reasons for these changes.

Hitler becomes Chancellor

Source 1

'The Dead Parliament', by German artist John Heartfield. This picture is a photomontage, made by cutting up and rearranging photographs. It appeared in a Communist magazine in October 1930. It shows an empty Reichstag with nothing to do because the President was using Article 48 of the constitution to make laws without consulting it. On the President's desk are an army helmet with a swastika, a top hat and a bishop's mitre, suggesting that the President was influenced by pro-Nazi army officers, businessmen and the Church.

Das tote Parlament

DAS BLIEB VOM JAHRE 1848 ÜBRIG!
So sieht der Reichstag aus, der am 13. Oktober eröffnet wird.

Brüning's government

From 1930 to 1932 President Hindenburg and Chancellor Brüning governed Germany by making decrees. This was not a democratic way of governing Germany, but it was not illegal. Article 48 of the constitution allowed the President to do so. However, it did mean that democracy started to die during these years. It also meant that friends of the President, such as army officers, had more influence over law-making than the elected Reichstag. Source 1 is a critical comment on this.

Despite the backing of President Hindenburg, Brüning was very unpopular. His policies not only failed to end the Depression. They also angered many people in high places, such as businessmen and landowners. Taking advantage of Brüning's unpopularity, a senior army officer, General Schleicher, persuaded Hindenburg to sack him. Another Centre Party politician, Franz von Papen, took his place.

Papen's government

Papen had only 68 supporters in the Reichstag, so he held an election in July 1932, hoping to get more. The result was a disappointment for him (see Source 4 on page 51). The Nazis were now the biggest party in the Reichstag, and Hitler demanded the post of Chancellor for himself.

Hindenburg refused to make Hitler Chancellor. He mistrusted him, and thought the Nazis were too violent to be given power. Instead, he asked Papen to stay in office. He would use his power to make decrees to put Papen's decisions into effect.

This did not help Papen. When the new Reichstag met, it voted on whether it had confidence in him. Thirty-two said yes but 513 said no. Faced with this massive vote of no-confidence, Papen arranged yet another election for November, still hoping to get a Reichstag which supported him.

Schleicher takes over

The November election gave Papen even fewer seats, so he went to Hindenburg with a new plan. He suggested closing down the Reichstag, governing by decree, and using the army to crush any opposition. Hindenburg agreed.

At this point, however, General Schleicher threw an obstacle in Papen's way. He told Hindenburg that Papen's plan would provoke the Nazis, Communists and other extremists into using armed force against the government.

Source 2

A demonstration by uniformed Social Democrats (on the left) is attacked by uniformed Nationalists in lorries (right) in Berlin in 1932.

In short, there would be a civil war. The picture above (Source 2) shows the kind of scene he might have had in mind. He warned that the army could not be relied upon to stop it. As no government can exist without the army's support, Papen had to resign. Schleicher himself became Chancellor.

Schleicher lasted only two months. The Reichstag would not agree to his decisions. So, like Brüning and Papen, he asked Hindenburg to make laws for him by decree. Unsurprisingly, Hindenburg was suspicious. Only weeks before, Schleicher had warned of civil war if Papen governed by decree. Now he was wanting the same thing. Hindenburg refused and asked Schleicher to resign.

Hitler takes power

Two Chancellors had come and gone in only eight months. Hindenburg now had no alternative. He had to offer the job to the leader of the largest party – Hitler. He made Hitler Chancellor on 30 January 1933.

Did Hitler gain power legally?

You read on page 41 that Hitler decided to stay within the law when he came out of prison. Nine years later, he became Chancellor after winning a series of elections and being offered the job by Germany's President. But was this as legal as it sounds? Study the accounts of Nazi election campaigns in Sources 3–8, and make up your own mind.

Source 3

From a moderate Berlin newspaper, *Vossische Zeitung*, 28 July 1932.

28 July 1932: near Stettin, SA raiders invaded a Social Democrat rally and challenged the speaker to take back a remark he had made about Adolf Hitler.... They attacked people in the audience with chairs, injuring ten of them critically and making the meeting hall a shambles.

Source 4

A report on Nazi campaign methods in the 1930 elections, written by the Prussian Ministry of the Interior.

* **tattoos** Military parades.

Propaganda squads stay in a certain place for several days and try to win the local population to the (Nazi) movement through the most varied forms of entertainment such as concerts, sports days, tattoos* and even church parades. In other places an outside propaganda speaker is stationed for a certain time; with a car at his disposal, he travels throughout the surrounding district. Nazi theatre groups travelling from place to place serve the same purpose.

Source 5

A description of the election campaign in 1932 in Kurt Ludecke, *I Knew Hitler*, 1938.

* **Beobachter** and **Angriff** Nazi newspapers.

As I walked through the Berlin streets, the Party flag was everywhere in evidence. Huge posters...and Nazi slogans screamed from windows and kiosks.... Passers-by wore tiny lapel emblems; uniformed men elbowed their way through the crowds, the swastika circling their brawny arms. *Beobachter** and *Angriff** were piled high.

Source 6

A battle between Communists (foreground) and Nazi Stormtroopers (background) who attacked a communist election meeting in Berlin in 1932.

Source 7

Arnold Brecht, *Prelude to Silence. The End of the German Republic*, 1944. The author was a senior government official in 1932. He was an opponent of the Nazi Party.

1 August: [Assassination] attempts in Königsberg on the Prussian District President, and on a city councillor, who died from his wounds. Two Communists and two leaders of the Social Democrat Party seriously wounded. Bombs thrown at three newspaper buildings.

2 August: Bombs planted in ten towns in Holstein, pistol shots fired in

Marienberg, and hand grenades thrown....

3 August: The Mayor of Norgau shot dead....

4 August: Two police officers killed in Gleiwitz. Fire bombs thrown at a department store in Ortelsberg....

5 August: Bomb plot against the Reichsbank branch office in Lötzen.

6 August: Hand grenades thrown at a chemist's shop in Lyck, pistol shots at a Communist home in Tilsit....

7 August: Leader of the *Reichsbanner** organisation shot to death in Lötzen, hand grenades thrown at a Catholic newspaper office.

9 August: More than twenty attempts with grenades, bombs and pistols in Silesia and East Prussia. A Nazi torn to death by his own grenade in Reichenbach.... A Communist, called Pietzruch, brutally murdered in the presence of his mother by five Nazis.

* **Reichsbanner**
The uniformed, paramilitary wing of the Social Democratic Party – equivalent to the Nazi SA.

Source 8

This cartoon appeared in a Social Democrat magazine in 1932. The caption said, 'Hitler's interpretation of the word "legal".'

Questions

1   Look at Source 1.
    a Explain in your own words the meaning of (i) the empty seats, (ii) the number §48, (iii) the title of the picture, 'The Dead Parliament'.
    b What do you think John Heartfield wanted people to think when they saw the picture? Explain your answer.

2   Look carefully at Source 8.
    a How does the cartoonist suggest that Hitler used (i) legal methods (ii) illegal methods in the election campaigns?
    b Do you think the cartoonist wanted us to think that Hitler took power legally or illegally? Explain your answer.
    c Judging by Sources 3–7, do you think the cartoonist was being fair? Explain your answer fully, referring to the sources.

Unit 4 Review

Study the photographs below, then answer the questions which follow.

Source 1   Surrounded by cheering supporters, Hitler leaves the presidential palace after being sworn in as Germany's new Chancellor.

Source 2   Three months after leaving prison, Hitler refounds the Nazi Party.

Source 3   After winning 95 new seats in a general election, 107 brown-shirted Nazis take their places in the Reichstag.

Source 4   Tired, dispirited, out-of-work men eating in a charity soup kitchen in Berlin at the start of the Great Depression.

Questions

1   The photographs above were taken between 1925 and 1933. Using Unit 4 of this book for information, identify the year in which each one was taken.

2   Look at the photographs in chronological order. Now write three paragraphs which explain the connections between each one.

3   If the events shown in the second picture had not happened, would the events shown in the third and fourth pictures have taken place? Explain your answer.

Unit 5 · Democracy destroyed: Hitler becomes a dictator, 1933–34

Hitler became Chancellor of Germany on 30 January 1933. When he won another election in March, the Reichstag gave him the power to make laws without its consent. He quickly used this power to outlaw all other parties and organisations which might oppose him. He then put Nazis in control of every important body. Hitler thus became a dictator and Germany became a one-party state.

A dictator is a ruler who has sole and complete power. To make sure he kept it, he murdered anyone in the Nazi Party who might oppose him. Then, when President Hindenburg died in 1934, he made himself President as well as Chancellor. From then on he ruled Germany as its 'Führer' – a leader with supreme power.

This Unit looks at the process by which Hitler became a dictator and asks how it was possible for him to destroy the democratic system so quickly and completely.

'Hitler – Germany's Doom.' An illustration from an anti-Nazi pamphlet of 1933 shows the German people being led into the grave of German democracy.

The Nazi seizure of power

Although he was now Chancellor, Hitler's power was limited. Only three of eleven government ministers were Nazis. The Nazi Party had less than half the seats in the Reichstag. And just as Hindenburg had made Hitler Chancellor, so he could sack him if he failed to govern effectively. Hitler therefore looked for ways of increasing his power.

He began by arranging another election, hoping to get a majority of seats in the Reichstag. Using every kind of propaganda, as well as mass meetings and parades, the Nazis aimed for a big win. They also continued to use violence against other parties, especially the Communists.

The Reichstag Fire

The Nazi election campaign was given a boost on 27 February 1933 by an unexpected event. The Reichstag burnt down. A Communist called Marinus van der Lubbe was caught at the scene of the blaze.

Historians disagree about how the fire started. Some say that the Nazis started it, and accused van der Lubbe so that they could blame the Communists. Others believe van der Lubbe's claim that he acted alone.

Whoever started the fire, it was very convenient for the Nazis. Hitler claimed it was the start of a Communist plot against the government. He asked President Hindenburg for extra powers to deal with the plot. Believing that Germany was in danger, Hindenburg issued a 'Law for the Protection of the People and State'.

Source 1

The Reichstag still on fire on the morning of 28 February 1933.

This emergency law suspended parts of the constitution (see Source 4 on page 60). That allowed the Nazis to smash the Communist election campaign. Stormtroopers arrested 4,000 Communists, shut down the Communist newspapers, and broke up Communist meetings (see Source 2).

Source 2

Nazi Stormtroopers beat up a Communist during the 1933 election campaign.

The election of 5 March 1933

The election took place on 5 March. It gave the Nazis more Reichstag seats than ever before. But, as you can see from Source 3, they still did not have a majority. Moreover, the Communists still had 81 seats, while the Centre and Socialist seats were almost unchanged. This was not what Hitler had wanted.

Source 3

Statistisches Jahrbuch für das Deutsche Reich ('Statistical Yearbook for the German Reich'), 1933.

Results of the March 1933 elections	
Nazi Party	288 seats
Social Democratic Party	120 seats
Communist Party	81 seats
Centre Party	74 seats
Nationalist Party	52 seats
Other parties	32 seats

Hitler overcame this setback with the help of the Nationalist Party. He persuaded it to join forces with the Nazi Party. Their 52 seats, added to the Nazis' 288 seats, amounted to just over half the Reichstag.

The Enabling Law

Although he now had a majority in the Reichstag, Hitler was still not satisfied. He wanted the Reichstag to pass an 'Enabling Law'. This would give him the power for the next four years to make laws without having to ask it for approval. To put it another way, the Enabling Law would give Hitler the power of a dictator.

This would require a change to Germany's constitution. But the constitution said that it could only be changed if at least two-thirds of the Reichstag voted to do so. As Hitler only had half, not two-thirds of the seats, he had to persuade at least another 91 members to vote for the Enabling Law. Source 5 describes one of the ways in which he did so. The result was that 444 members voted in favour – just over two-thirds. Only 94 voted against. Hitler thus became a dictator, and Germany ceased to be a democracy.

A 'seizure of power'?

Many historians describe the way in which Hitler strengthened his position early in 1933 as a 'seizure of power'. But, as you have read, his power was increased by the passing of laws. So is it correct to say that he seized power? Let us look at the laws and at how they were made. The first one was the Law for the Protection of People and State. This suspended the following sections of the constitution:

Source 4

Heinrich Oppenheimer, *The Constitution of the German Republic*, 1923.

* **inviolable** Cannot be taken away.
* **assemble** To hold public meetings.

Article 114 Personal freedom is inviolable*....
Article 115 The home of every German is a sanctuary for him and is inviolable.
Article 117 The secrecy of correspondence, as well as the secrecy of postal, telegraphic and telephonic communications is inviolable.
Article 118 Every German is entitled within the limits of the general law to express his opinions by word of mouth, writing, printing, pictures, or otherwise.... There is no censorship....
Article 123 All Germans have the right...to assemble* peaceably and unarmed.
Article 124 All Germans have the right to form societies or associations....
Article 153 Property is guaranteed by the Constitution.

When the Reichstag met to vote on the Enabling Law on 24 March, it did so in an opera house in Berlin. The Reichstag building had been put out of action by the fire. The atmosphere in which the members met was later described by one of the Social Democrats who was there on that day:

Source 5

Wilhelm Hoegner, *Der Schwierige Aussenseiter* ('The Difficult Outsider'), 1963.

The wide square in front of the Kroll Opera House was crowded with dark masses of people. We were received with wild choruses: 'We want the Enabling Act!' Youths with swastikas on their chests eyed us insolently, blocking our way, in fact made us run the gauntlet, calling us names like 'Centre pig', 'Marxist sow'. The Kroll Opera House was crawling with armed SA and SS men.... When we Social Democrats had taken up our seats at the extreme left, SA and SS men lined up at the exits and along the walls behind us in a semicircle. Their expressions boded no good.

The Enabling Law, which was passed that day, stated that:

Source 6

Reichsgesetzblatt ('Reich Law Gazette'), 1933.

* **Reich Cabinet** The ministers, headed by Hitler, who ran the various government departments.

Article 1 ...the Reich Cabinet* is authorised to enact laws.
Article 2 The laws enacted by the Reich Cabinet may deviate from the Constitution....
Article 3 The laws enacted by the Reich Cabinet shall be prepared by the Chancellor.... They come into effect, unless otherwise specified, upon the day following their publication....
Article 5 This law comes into effect on the day of its publication. It ceases to be valid on 1 April 1937....

This Nazi poster for the March 1933 election shows President Hindenburg (left) and Hitler, the new Chancellor, asking voters to 'fight with us for peace and equal rights'.

DER **MARSCHALL** UND DER **GEFREITE**

'KÄMPFEN MIT UNS FÜR FRIEDEN UND GLEICHBERECHTIGUNG

Questions

1 Study Source 4, then answer these questions:
   a Find six things that the constitution said were 'inviolable'.
   b Give examples of 'personal freedom' (Article 114).
   c What is censorship (Article 118)?
   d Why might people want to 'assemble' (Article 123)?
   e What sorts of 'societies or associations' (Article 124) might people want to form?

2 Describe in your own words how a person's life might have been affected by the suspension of these parts of the constitution.

3 Study Source 5. What pressures were there on Centre Party and Social Democrat members to vote for the Enabling Law?

4 Study the Enabling Law (Source 6). Why, despite the pressures on them to vote for it, do you think that 96 Socialist members voted against it?

5 Judging by the text and sources in this section, do you think that Hitler 'seized' power, or was he just given it? Explain your answer.

Bringing Germany into line

Now that Hitler could make his own laws, he reorganised the German political system so that every part of it was under Nazi control. He called this *Gleichschaltung*, which means 'bringing into line'.

The states are brought into line

Germany was a federation of eighteen states (see page 19). Each had its own parliament, police and laws. On 31 March 1933 Hitler closed down the state parliaments. Each was then reorganised so that it had the same composition as the Reichstag. This meant that the Nazis were now the largest party in all the state parliaments.

On 7 April Hitler appointed state governors to each state. All eighteen governors were Nazis. They had the power to appoint and to dismiss state officials. They also had the power to make state laws.

Later, on 30 January 1934, Hitler would abolish the state parliaments.

The trade unions are brought into line

Next to be brought into line were the trade unions. On 2 May 1933, Nazis broke into trade-union offices all over the country (see Source 1) and arrested thousands of union officials. The unions were then merged into a 'German Labour Front'. At its head was a Nazi.

The parties are brought into line

Lastly, the parties were brought into line. On 10 May Nazis occupied the offices of the Social Democratic Party, destroyed its newspapers and confiscated its funds. Two weeks later they confiscated all the property and funds of the Communist Party. The other, smaller parties suffered the

Source 1

Nazi Stormtroopers occupy the offices of the German trade unions in Munich on 2 May 1933.

same fate in June. One by one their offices were closed down and their leaders arrested.

By July 1933 only one party was still in existence – the Nazi Party. On 14 July Hitler made a law stating that the Nazi Party was the only party allowed in Germany, and forbidding the creation of any other party. Germany thus became a one-party state.

Bringing life into line

What did this all mean for the people involved? What were the human consequences of being 'brought into line'?

For thousands of people, the immediate consequence was their arrest. Source 2 describes what often happened next.

Source 2

From a pamphlet written and distributed by a group of banned Communists in April 1933.

> **Listen! Read! Pass it on! Hitler's Crimes!**
> In Berlin alone thousands of Social Democratic and Communist officials were dragged from their beds at night...and led away to SA barracks. There they were worked over with boot and whip, beaten with steel rods and rubber truncheons until they collapsed unconscious and blood spurted under their skin. Many were forced to drink castor oil or had urine directed into their mouths; others had their bones broken. Working class officials were tortured to death and public figures slaughtered savagely by these and similar methods of torture.

The Nazis denied torturing their prisoners. Hoping to prove that they treated prisoners humanely, they invited news reporters to one of their prison camps near Berlin. Source 3 is typical of the scenes which the reporters photographed.

Source 3

Social Democratic members of the state parliament of Prussia in Orienanen prison camp near Berlin, shortly after their arrest on 10 August 1933.

One of those who spent time in prison was Stefan Lorant, a newspaper editor. Allowed paper and pencil by his guards, he kept a diary while he was in prison in 1933. He published it after his release and later escape from Germany. This extract helps to explain how the Nazis were able to 'bring into line' so many people so quickly:

Source 4

Stefan Lorant, *I Was Hitler's Prisoner. Leaves from a Prison Diary*, 1935.

27 March 1933

New prisoners are continually brought in, day and night…. A farmer at whose house two useless rifles were discovered. A workman who had said in a pub 'Hitler can't help us, either'. A painter who was a member of the Communist Party. A farmer who was supposed to have hidden explosives. These are the political prisoners.

The reason they are here? 'We have been informed against, that's all it is', is their answer. In New Germany, whenever anyone wants to get rid of a competitor in trade, or give an enemy something to think about, or revenge himself on a lover, he simply denounces* the person in an anonymous letter to the Political Police.

* **denounces** Informs against; accuses.

The risk of being 'denounced' altered people's behaviour, at home as well as in public. Source 5 describes one new form of behaviour:

Source 5

Arnold Brecht, *The Political Education of Arnold Brecht. An Autobiography, 1884–1970*, 1970. The author was a senior government official who lost his job when the Nazis came to power.

A favourite sport of irregular groups of National Socialists was searching apartments for papers and books with suspicious contents. Houses from whose chimneys rose a sudden short burst of smoke aroused suspicion that papers were being burned there. People therefore avoided burning papers and instead took the trouble to tear them into thousands of little pieces and flush them down the toilet.

A similar picture emerges from Source 6. It is from a book written anonymously by someone who left Germany soon after the process of 'bringing into line' began.

Source 6

A German Jewish scientist, *Why I Left Germany*, 1934.

An inconsidered word uttered before a stranger might mean house-searching, legal prosecution, or even a concentration camp…. A remark in a private letter abroad, one word on the telephone might suffice. Private letters and telephone calls were under constant supervision…. In trams and in the underground, in all public places in fact, it was necessary to avoid entering into conversation with strangers.

Many Germans supported the Nazis and had no objection to being 'brought into line'. This can be seen in Source 7. It comes from the diary of a keen Nazi supporter.

Source 7

Elizabeth von Stahlenberg, *Nazi Lady. The Diaries of Elizabeth von Stahlenberg, 1933–1948*, 1978.

I *cannot* understand politics! Half the trade union leaders…have been arrested. I'm sure there's a good reason…. Anyhow, the workers are to be protected, even without their unions…. If one thinks about it, then it is right that the unions should hand over power to the government. If we're to get anywhere in the world, then we have to do it as a nation. As Germans first and foremost.

Source 8

Even the police were 'brought into line'. Here, Prussian policemen parade in Berlin in 1933, carrying Nazi flags and giving the Nazi salute.

Questions

1   Sources 2 and 3 give very different views of Nazi prisons in 1933.
    a Why can neither source be trusted to give a completely accurate picture of conditions in prison?
    b Bearing in mind your answer to question **a**, which of the two sources do you think is most likely to be a more accurate picture of Nazi prisons? Explain your answer.

2   Sources 4 and 5 were written by people who fled from Germany in 1933 to escape the Nazis. Does this affect their value as evidence of Nazi rule in 1933? Explain your answer.

3   Using the sources and text in this section, describe how the 'bringing into line' of Germany in 1933-34 changed:
    a the political system of Germany
    b the lives of Germans who did not support the Nazis.

The Night of the Long Knives

Source 1

An article in a German magazine, tracing the development of the SA uniform from the foundation of the SA in 1921 up to 1933. (Note: the SA were banned from wearing uniforms for part of 1932.)

By 1934 Hitler had wiped out most of his opponents. His only rivals left were in the Nazi Party itself, and in the SA - the Stormtroopers.

The SA

The SA, as you have read, was the brown-shirted military wing of the Nazi Party. Containing large numbers of hooligans and street-fighters, the SA had helped Hitler take power by terrorising his opponents.

Many of the SA expected to benefit from Nazi rule. The unemployed among them wanted jobs. The leaders wanted positions of power. Others expected Hitler to put into effect the economic parts of the Nazi programme (see line 12 of Source 2 on page 37). They wanted what they called a 'second revolution'.

Ernst Röhm, the leader of the SA, talked of a bigger role for his men. He wanted to merge the SA with the regular army, with both under his control. This alarmed Hitler. A merger of the two would make Röhm the most powerful man in Germany. It also alarmed the generals of the army. A merger would reduce their own power.

The Night of the Long Knives

Hitler could not afford to lose the support of the army generals. Nor could he risk allowing Röhm to gain so much power. On Hitler's orders, Röhm and other SA leaders were arrested on the night of 30 June 1934. They were taken to prison and shot. Over the following week, hundreds of other SA leaders were murdered, along with dozens of other possible rivals to Hitler. The killings were done by the black-shirted SS.

Some Nazis described the killings as 'the Night of the Long Knives'. Others called them 'the blood purge'. Whatever they called it, the

Source 2

Conan Fisher, *Stormtroopers. A Social, Economic and Ideological Analysis, 1929–35,* 1983.

Membership of the SA	
August 1929	30,000
November 1930	60,000
January 1931	100,000
January 1932	291,000
August 1932	445,000
January 1933	425,000
August 1933	2,000,000
January 1934	3,000,000

importance of the event was the same. Hitler had wiped out the only real threat to his power. In so doing he had gained the support of the army generals. He was now stronger than ever.

Why was the SA dangerous to Hitler?

Hitler could not have gained power without the help of the SA. So why did he turn his back on the force to which he owed his position?

The SA had helped to bring Hitler to power by using violence against his opponents. But once he was in power, Hitler had less need of their violent methods. Nevertheless, they continued to act violently. This was an embarrassment to Hitler, as Source 3 suggests:

Source 3

From a letter written by the Minister of the Interior, the government minister responsible for the police, in October 1933.

> New infringements…by the SA have been reported again and again during the past weeks. Above all, SA leaders and men have carried out police actions for which they had no authority…. The infringements and excesses must now cease once and for all.

The contrast between the SA and the rest of the Nazi Party grew after 1933. One SA member later explained why there was such a contrast:

Source 4

Johannes Beck (ed.), *Terror und Hoffnung in Deutschland* ('Terror and Hope in Germany') *1933–1945*, 1980.

> We thought: *we* created that (Nazi government), *we* prepared the way, why shouldn't we carry on with it?… We simply laughed at the party members running around…after 1933 – we didn't take them seriously. The politicians, the party officials were not at all popular with us…. We were the *fighting troop*. And we didn't want anyone to take over from us.

At the heart of the problem lay Röhm's ambition to merge the SA with the army. Röhm's views were recorded by a Nazi, Hermann Rauschning, who discussed the future of the SA with him over lunch in 1934:

Source 5

Hermann Rauschning, *Hitler Speaks*, 1939.

* **his scars** Röhm had scars on his face after being wounded in the First World War.
* **reactionaries** People who dislike change.

> His scars* were scarlet with excitement. He had drunk a few glasses of wine in quick succession.
>   'Adolf is a swine', he swore. 'He will give us all away. He only associates with the reactionaries* now. His old friends aren't good enough for him. Getting matey with the…generals. They're his cronies now.
>   He was jealous and hurt.
>   'The generals are a lot of old fogies. I am the nucleus of a new army….'

Questions

1 What changes in the SA can you see in Sources 1 and 2?

2 Using the photographs on pages 54, 59 and 62, give examples of ways in which the SA helped Hitler to gain power.

3 Look at Sources 2–5. Find as many reasons as you can why Hitler wanted to get rid of Röhm and other leaders of the SA.

Hitler the Führer

Only weeks after the Night of the Long Knives, Hitler increased his power still further. When 87-year-old President Hindenburg died, Hitler combined the posts of President and Chancellor, and gave himself the job. His new title was 'Führer and Reich Chancellor'.

On the same day, 2 August 1934, every soldier in the German army swore an oath: 'I will give unconditional obedience to Adolf Hitler, the Führer of the German nation and people….' In taking the oath, the only people who still had the power to oppose Hitler – soldiers with guns – had sworn total obedience to him. Thus, eighteen months after becoming Chancellor, Hitler had supreme, unchallenged power in Germany.

Source 1

A German family giving the 'German Salute'. The family was originally from Lithuania, and had recently emigrated to Germany. They were photographed here in 1940 at a ceremony in which they were given German citizenship.

The cult of the Führer

Hitler's title 'Führer' has several meanings. Chiefly it means 'leader' but it can also mean 'guide', 'manager' and 'pilot'.

To millions of Germans in the 1930s, Hitler was all these things. They saw him not just as the head of the government but also as national leader, law-giver and commander. His importance was such that all public employees had, by law, to greet others with the 'German salute' (see Source 1) while saying 'Heil Hitler'.

Most Germans gave the 'German salute' and said 'Heil Hitler', whether they were Nazis or not. One reason for doing so can be seen in Source 2:

Source 2

From the memoirs of a German Communist, Karl Billinger, *All Quiet in Germany*, 1935.

* **Brown Shirts** A commonly used name for the SA, taken from the colour of their uniform.

For three months I had managed to avoid saluting the swastika flag.... You could always steer clear of SA parades and demonstrations by turning off into a side street or restaurant. I tried it once too often, however.... I caught sight of an approaching procession of Nazi nurses, carrying banners. Without stopping to think, I turned my back on it and walked in the opposite direction, only to face four Brown Shirts* crossing towards me from the other side of the street.

'Trying to get out of it?' said one. 'Arm up! And now – ?'

'Heil Hitler', I said.

I could have spat at myself as I strode past the procession with arm uplifted.

There were dozens of other ways in which Germans were expected to demonstrate their loyalty to the Führer. Source 3 describes some of them:

Source 3

A German-Jewish scientist, *Why I Left Germany*, 1934.

* **edelweiss** A small flower, like a daisy, that grows in the Alps.

On the 20 April the new Chancellor celebrated his forty-fourth birthday.... Hitler's picture was in the papers, in the shop windows, on the pavements; Hitler cakes were displayed in the confectioners' shops, his biography in book and stationers' shops. Men collecting money were posted at every street corner. They were selling edelweiss* emblems.

'Hitler's birthday fund! The leader's favourite flower!'

Most people in the street wore this emblem in their button-holes.

To some people, the cult of the Führer seemed almost religious. This was the impression that a Dutch visitor to Germany gained in 1934:

Source 4

Hendrik de Leeuw, *Sinful Cities of the Western World*, 1945.

* **Hakenkreuz** Swastika. Literally, it means 'crooked cross'.
* **Deutschland song** The German national anthem.

I watched a Hitler demonstration in the German capital.... Hundreds of thousands took the strange Hitler oath that would bind them forever, they believed, to *Der Führer* and the *Hakenkreuz**. When the last word of the leader had died down and the band had started the Deutschland song*....I beheld a people aroused to an orgy of emotion. When the music stopped...the leader spoke again – 'And now we are coming to the oath, which repeat after me, "I swear to be true to Adolf Hitler, our Führer, and swear obedience"'. Then all took the oath in absolute solemnity.

According to Source 5, even animals were affected by the Hitler cult. It is taken from an article in a Nazi newspaper. It describes what happened when a woman teacher visited the home of Baroness Freytag-Loringhoven, who owned a talking dog:

Source 5

Schwarzes Korps (the newspaper of the Nazi SS), 31 July 1935

* **vivisection** Experiments carried out on living animals.

The Baroness prompted my husband to put a difficult question to the dog. My husband asked, 'Who is Adolf Hitler?' We were deeply moved to hear the answer 'My Führer' out of the mouth of the creature.

When the teacher told this story to a class of Nazi students, one of the class called out, 'This is in abominably bad taste. You are misusing the Führer's name.'

To which the teacher replied, 'This clever animal knows that Adolf Hitler has caused laws to be passed against vivisection*... and out of gratitude his small canine brain recognises Adolf Hitler as his Führer.'

Finally, to make sure that the Hitler cult reached every part of the country, official portraits of Hitler were mass-produced in 1936. They were put up in school rooms, government offices, law courts and every other kind of public place. Source 6 is a typical example of these pictures.

Source 6

This photograph was taken in the mosque in Berlin in January 1939. A Muslim cleric is celebrating the end of Ramadan. Behind him is an official portrait of Hitler. To his right is the swastika flag.

Questions

1 Sources 1–6 show different aspects of the 'Hitler cult'.
   a What does the word 'cult' mean?
   b Give at least three examples of the methods, mentioned in these sources, which were used to create the 'Hitler cult'.
   c What seem to have been the purposes of the 'Hitler cult'?

2 Read Source 5 again.
   a Assume for the moment that the dog really could talk. Why do you think the Baroness trained it to say 'My Führer'.
   b Dogs do not talk, so this story is not entirely true. Does this affect the story's value as evidence of the Hitler cult? Explain your answer.

Unit 5 Review

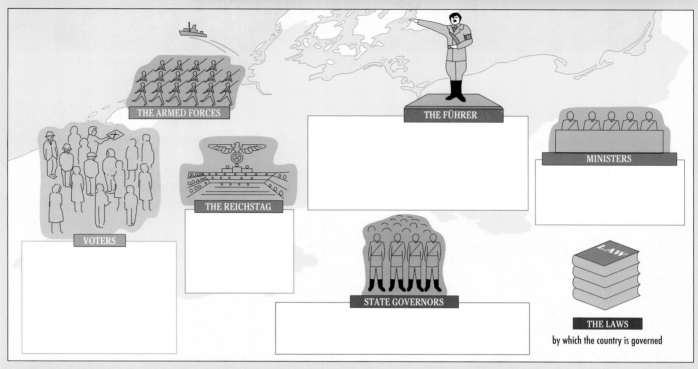

The German system of government after 1934

Questions

1 On a copy of the diagram above, put the following descriptions into the boxes which they match:

Anyone over 20 has the right to vote in:
• one-party elections for the Reichstag
• plebiscites, arranged at the wish of the Führer, to show whether they agree with decisions he has made.

Has the power to:
• make laws
• summon and dismiss the Reichstag
• appoint and dismiss all ministers, army officers, state governors, party and government officials
• decide foreign policy, declare war and make peace.

18 Nazi governors appointed by the Führer:
• full power over the state governments and all local officials.
• controlled by the Minister of the Interior.

Consists of ministers appointed by the Führer: they put his decisions into effect.

600 deputies representing the Nazi Party. They can discuss new laws but cannot vote against them.

2 Now link the boxes with arrows (as in the diagram on page 18) to show the connections between them.

3 Compare your completed diagram with that on page 18. Then, in two columns on a separate sheet of paper,
a list any similarities between the two systems of government
b list any differences between the two systems of government.

4 In what ways does your list show that Hitler destroyed the democratic system of the Weimar Republic?

Unit 6 · The purposes of dictatorship: life in Nazi Germany (1)

A spectacular example of Nazi power and control: 100,000 men, carrying 32,000 flags, march past Hitler at the 1937 Nuremberg rally. Above them, 150 searchlights create a 'cathedral of light'.

Hitler had three main purposes. The first was to rebuild Germany's ruined economy. The second was to make Germany a powerful nation again. The third was to create a 'pure German' society by getting rid of racial minority groups, especially Jews.

Following these three aims changed the lives of millions of people. The greatest changes were felt by Germany's 600,000 Jews. They were deprived of their rights, driven out of their jobs, and treated in every way as an 'inferior race'. Also greatly affected were millions of unemployed, who were put to work in job schemes and work camps.

To achieve these aims quickly, Hitler required complete obedience from the German people. Everybody thus found that they were being controlled more and more by the state authorities – the Party, the police and the government.

This Unit looks at how people's lives were changed by all these developments. You may feel that some changes were for the better. But when you have finished reading, you may have reason to think that many were for the worse.

Work and bread

At least six million Germans were out of work when Hitler came to power. He had promised these people 'work and bread' in the election campaigns of 1932–33. Now one of his priorities had to be to give them jobs.

The National Labour Service

Fortunately for Hitler, several job-creation schemes had already been started by previous governments. One was the National Labour Service (*Reichsarbeitsdienst*, or RAD). This gave young men jobs on projects needing large amounts of manual labour, such as planting new forests or digging ditches on farms (see Source 1).

Soon after coming to power, Hitler took over the Labour Service and expanded it. The men in it were put into uniform and sent to work camps. There they received pocket money rather than wages, and did military drill as well as work. In 1935, a Reich Labour Service Law said that all men aged 18–25 must spend six months in the Labour Service. With hundreds of thousands of young Germans entering the work camps, the jobless figures dropped sharply.

Source 1

Men in the National Labour Service clearing a ditch on a farm in 1934.

Public work schemes

The Nazis also took over a road-building programme from the previous government. A law of June 1933 expanded the programme by ordering the creation of a network of motorways. This gave work to never fewer than 80,000 men over the next five years. At the same time, a Law to Reduce Unemployment gave government grants for building new homes, schools, hospitals and other public services. To make sure that this gave work to as many people as possible, this law said that all such building must be done by hand.

Rearmament

Another of Hitler's priorities after seizing power was to build up Germany's armed forces (see page 86). This had a big impact on the unemployment figures. From 1935 onwards, all 18- to 25-year-olds had to do military service for two years. The armed forces thus grew from 100,000 in 1933 to 1,400,000 in 1939, cutting over a million from the unemployment registers.

How successful were Nazi employment policies?

A glance at Source 2 suggests that Hitler was very successful in providing the jobless with work. Such figures, however, tell us nothing about the *kind* of work he provided. Sources 3–5 give a very different picture.

Source 2

Unemployment in Germany, 1933–39, *International Labour Review*, International Labour Office, Geneva, 1933–39.

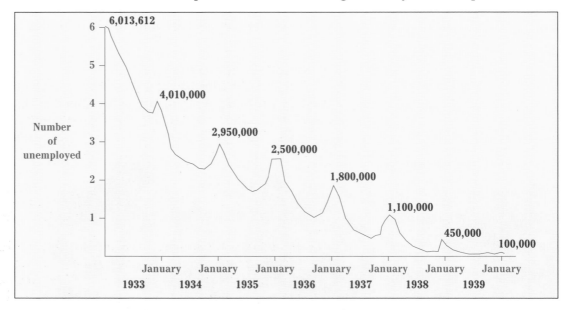

Source 3

SOPADE-Berichte ('Reports of the Social Democratic Party in Exile'), 1938. This was a collection of reports by agents of the banned Social Democrats, in exile in Czechoslovakia.

* **drill** See Source 5.
* **Pf** Pfennigs, or pennies. 25 Pf was roughly the same as 40 pence today.

> Saxony, April/May 1938: The daily programme of the labour service camp at Beiersfeld/Erzebirge 9/165 looks like this: 4.45 a.m. get up. 4.50 gymnastics. 5.15 wash, make beds. 5.30 coffee break. 5.50 parade. 6.00 march to building site. Work till 14.30 with 30 minutes break for breakfast. 15.00 lunch. 15.30–18.00 drill*. 18.10–18.45 instruction. 18.45–19.15 cleaning and mending. 19.15 parade. 19.30 announcements. 19.45 supper. 20.00–21.30 sing song or other leisure activities. 22.00 lights out. The day is thus filled with duties…. The wage is 25 Pf* a day.

Work on the road-building programme was better paid than work in the Labour Service. But, as Source 4 suggests, it too had disadvantages. It is from an account by a German journalist of a train journey he took in 1936, then aged 15. Sitting opposite him were two road workers, telling another passenger about their work:

Source 4

Bernt Engelmann, *In Hitler's Germany. Everyday Life in the Third Reich*, 1988.

> We work outdoors in all kinds of weather, shovelling dirt for 51 Pfennigs an hour. Then there are the deductions and voluntary contributions they take automatically, and 15 Pfennigs a day for a straw mattress in a draughty wooden barracks, and 35 Pfennigs for what they ladle out of a cauldron and call dinner – slop you wouldn't touch, I guarantee it.
>
> I'm trained as a printer (*said the second worker*). In the summer of '33 I lost my job. I collected the dole until the spring of '34 – and that was a lot better than what I'm doing now. At least I was home, with my family, and now and then I could pick up some odd jobs, or I could work in the garden. Now I'm in compulsory service with ten days' holiday a year….

Source 5

Young men in the National Labour Service doing military drill in 1935.

By 1939, as Source 2 shows, few Germans did not have a job. In many industries there was even a shortage of labour. The Nazis dealt with this new problem with even stricter measures. They accused anyone who was still unemployed of being 'work-shy'. An SS report described a campaign in 1937–38 against the 'work-shy'.

Source 6

Nuremberg Document NO-5591. The Nuremberg Documents were evidence used in the trial of Nazi leaders after the Second World War.

Vagrants, beggars, gypsies…were picked up by the criminal police and, finally, those wilfully refusing to earn a living were apprehended. Considerably in excess of 10,000 asocials* are currently undergoing a diet of work training in concentration camps.

* **asocials** A Nazi term meaning people who didn't 'fit in' with the rest of society.

Questions

1 **a** Study Source 2. Describe briefly how the unemployment figures changed between January 1933 and December 1939.
   b Which year shows the biggest fall in unemployment?
   c Judging by the information on page 73, what caused this fall?
   d Compare Source 2 with the graph on page 46. How long did it take after January 1933 for unemployment to fall back to its average level before the Depression?

2 Look back at Sources 3, 4 and 5 on page 48. They describe the lives of unemployed people in the Depression. What might these people have thought about the labour camp described in Source 3 of this section?

3 **a** Why were the workers in Source 4 complaining about their work?
   b Why might their work be considered preferable to the work in Source 3?

4 Hitler said, 'History will judge us according to whether we have succeeded in providing work'. Judging by the sources and information in this section, did he succeed? Explain your answer.

Racism

As you have read, Hitler and the Nazis believed that the German people were a *Volk*, or race. They thought that the Germans were distinct from other races and superior to them all. They wanted to preserve what they called the 'purity' of the German race by restricting the activities of other races. They especially wanted to restrict the activities of Jews.

The German Jews

Jews had lived in Germany for over a thousand years. Originally they were a Middle Eastern people. They had settled in Europe after being expelled from their homeland in ancient times. Over the centuries, hundreds of thousands of Jews had entered all levels of German society. A great many were shopkeepers, traders, bankers and business people. Many were doctors, lawyers, writers and artists.

Wherever they settled they were badly treated. In some places they were not allowed to own land. In others they had to live in a special part of town called a 'ghetto'. Sometimes they had to pay special taxes or wear distinctive clothes. From time to time they were attacked and murdered in mass killings known as 'pogroms'.

This ill-treatment of Jews is known as anti-semitism. It became one of the main features of Nazi Germany.

The attack on the Jews

The Nazis started to attack Jews as soon as they came to power. In April 1933 the SA organised a boycott of all Jewish-owned shops, cafés and businesses. They stood outside these places urging people not to enter. They painted the word *Jude* (Jew) on the windows (see Source 1), and beat up people who tried to enter.

Source 1

A Nazi Stormtrooper paints the word *Jude* (Jew) and the Jewish 'star of David' on a shop window in April 1933.

A week later, Hitler ordered the sacking from government jobs of anyone not of 'Aryan' (German) descent. Thousands of Jewish civil servants, lawyers and university teachers were immediately sacked.

During the summer of 1933 placards appeared outside shops, cafés, swimming pools, parks and many other public places throughout Germany, saying 'Jews not wanted' or 'Jews forbidden' (see Source 2).

The Nazi-controlled press ran hate campaigns against Jews. Nazi school authorities sacked Jewish teachers. Jewish actors and musicians were forbidden to perform in public. For the next two years, Jews everywhere in Germany were the victims of organised hate.

The Nuremberg Laws

In 1935 two new laws pushed anti-semitism to greater extremes. The Nuremberg Laws of 15 September 1935 barred Jews from being German citizens and took away some of their most basic rights. A series of laws over the next five years stripped Jews of every other right (see Source 3).

The Night of Broken Glass

Jews in many areas tried to resist the Nazis. All too often this led to worse treatment than before. In November 1938 a Jew shot dead a senior Nazi official. In retaliation, the SA carried out a campaign of terror against the Jewish population. It started on 10 November with the 'Night of Broken Glass', in which 10,000 Jewish shopkeepers had their windows smashed and the contents stolen. During the campaign, 91 Jews were murdered and 20,000 put into concentration camps*. Nearly 200 synagogues (Jewish churches) were burnt down. Finally, on 12 November, the Jews were ordered to pay a fine of one billion marks to the government.

* **concentration camps** High security prison camps used to imprison and kill oponents of the Nazis as well as racial and social 'undesirables'.

Source 2

This banner above a road leading into a Bavarian village said 'Jews are not wanted here'.

Why was racism so widespread in Nazi Germany?

Germany was a civilised country, and not everyone was a Nazi. So how was it possible for such terrible things to happen? Who was to blame?

Let us first consider the part played by Hitler's government. Between 1933 and 1945 it made no fewer than 45 decrees and laws against the Jews. Source 3 is a series of extracts from some of those laws, and Source 4 shows one of the methods used to enforce them:

Source 3

Reichsgesetzblatt ('Reich Law Gazette'), 1933–41.

A The Reich Law on Citizenship, 15 September 1935
A citizen of the Reich is a subject who is of German or kindred blood and who, through his conduct, shows that he wants and is fit to serve the German people and Reich faithfully.

B Law for the Protection of German Blood and Honour, 15 September 1935
1 Marriages between Jews and citizens of German or kindred blood are forbidden....
2 Sexual relations outside marriage between Jews and nationals of German or kindred blood are forbidden....

C Decree Regarding the Change of Family Names, 17 August 1938
Jews are allowed only certain first names.... Jews with first names different from those listed must register and use as signature the first name 'Israel' (for men) and 'Sara' (for women) in addition to their own first names.

D Decree to Eliminate the Jews from Economic Life, 12 November 1938
As of January 1939, Jews are forbidden to own shops,...to engage independently in any trade, or to offer for sale, advertise, or accept orders for goods or trade services at markets, fairs or exhibitions.

E Decree by the Reich Minister of Education, 16 November 1938
Jews are not permitted to attend German schools. They may only attend Jewish schools. All Jewish students not yet expelled from German schools must be expelled immediately.

F Decree by the Berlin Police, 3 December 1938
Jews are banned from all...theatres, shows, concert and lecture halls, museums, amusement places, sports fields, public and private bathing establishments, and several prominent Berlin streets....

G Decree Regarding Identification badges for Jews, 1 September 1941
Jews over six years of age must wear the 'Star of David' in public. The 'Star of David' is a black, six-pointed star on yellow material, as big as the palm of a hand, with the inscription 'Jew'.

Source 4

Every German had to carry identity passes. This pass belonged to 17-year-old Edith Baum. The letter J (for *Juden*) stamped on the first page showed that she was Jewish, as did the addition of 'Sara' to her name.

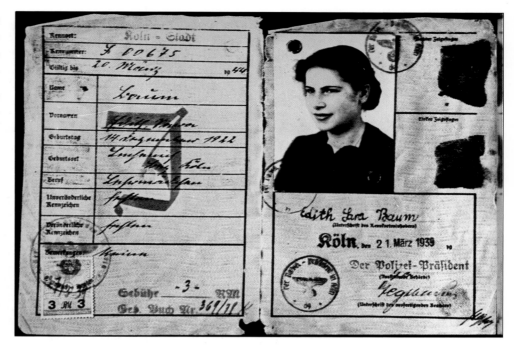

Making laws against Jews was only one way of restricting them. The Nazis also tried to change people's behaviour towards Jews. Young people especially were encouraged to hate Jews, with school lessons and textbooks putting across anti-semitic views. In Source 5, a Jewish woman who fled from Germany to live in the USA described how this was done in the class of her friend's daughter, Ada:

Source 5

Alice Salomon, *Character is Destiny*, an undated collection of memoirs kept in the Leo Baeck Institute, New York.

One day she came home humiliated. 'It was not so nice today'. What had happened? The teacher had sent the Aryan children to one side of the classroom, and the non-Aryans to the other. Then the teacher told the Aryans to study the appearance of the others and to point out the marks of their Jewish race. They stood separated as if by a gulf, children who had played together as friends the day before.

School textbooks and teaching materials were controlled by the government Ministry of Education. The government was thus able to put anti-semitic material into every classroom in Germany. Sources 6 and 7 are examples of such material.

Source 6

A homework exercise set in a German school in 1942, quoted in Carl Scheunes, *The Twisted Road to Auschwitz*, 1970

1 The Jewish race is much inferior to the Negro race.
2 All Jews have crooked legs, fat bellies, curly hair, and look untrustworthy.
3 The Jews were responsible for the First World War.
4 They are to blame for the armistice of 1918 and the Versailles Treaty.
5 They caused the Inflation*.
6 They brought about the downfall of the Roman Empire.
7 Marx* is a great criminal.
8 All Jews are Communists.
9 They are the rulers of Russia.

* **the Inflation**
  The hyperinflation of 1923.
* **Marx** Author of *The Communist Manifesto*.

Source 7

This is a page from a children's book published by the Nazi Party, called *Trust No Fox and No Jew*. It compares an Aryan man (left) 'who can work and fight' with a Jewish man (right) who, it says, is 'the greatest scoundrel in the whole Reich'.

Adults as well as children were bombarded with anti-semitic propaganda. One Nazi magazine told its readers:

Source 8
Racial Research Weekly, date unknown.

The Aryan hero must constantly be on his guard for the protection of the Aryan race and the well-being of the woman. We demand of a member of this noble race that he marry only a blue-eyed, oval-faced, red-cheeked and thin-nosed blonde woman. We demand that he take as his wife a virgin only. The blonde, blue-eyed Aryan man must by no means marry a dark-skinned girl of the Aryan type.

It was only a short step from reading in magazines about 'the protection of the Aryan race' to putting it into practice. Sources 9 and 10 show some of the results.

Source 9

Martha Dodd, *My Years in Germany*, 1939. The author was daughter of the United States Ambassador to Germany.

* **street car** Tram.

As we were coming out of the hotel we saw a crowd gathering...in the middle of the street. We stopped to find out what it was all about. There was a street car* in the centre of the road from which a young girl was being brutally pushed and shoved.... She looked ghastly. Her head had been shaved clean of hair and she was wearing a placard across her breast.... The placard said: 'I have offered myself to a Jew.'

Source 10

This photograph was taken in July 1933. Nazi Stormtroopers have arrested a woman and her Jewish partner. The sign around her neck says: I am the biggest pig of all. I only sleep with Jews!' The man's sign says 'I am a Jewish boy who always brings German girls to my room'.

Questions

1   Study Source 3 (laws A and B).
    a What does being a 'citizen' of your country mean?
    b What would you lose if you were deprived of your citizenship?

2   Describe how a Jewish person's life was changed by laws C–G.

3   Which of laws A–G might have made it easier for some people to treat Jews badly? Explain your answer.

4   Study Sources 5, 6 and 7. Explain what you think were the likely effects on schoolchildren of such materials.

5   How likely do you think adults were to be influenced by scenes like those in Sources 1 and 2, and by magazines such as Source 8?

6   Look back at your answers to questions 1–5. How much blame do you think should be attached to
    a individual Germans
    b the Nazi government
    for the ill-treatment of Jews in Germany between 1933 and 1939?

Control

One of the purposes of dictatorship was to give the Nazis control of people's lives. The more control they had, the more easily they could put their aims into effect. The job of controlling people thus became one of the main tasks of the Nazi state. It was done by two organisations: the Nazi Party and the police.

Police control

The Nazi police network was run by the SS. This was a branch of the SA which had started life as Hitler's bodyguard. Led by Heinrich Himmler, the SS helped Hitler to get rid of the SA leaders in the Night of the Long Knives. As a reward, Hitler made the SS independent of the SA. Two years later he gave Himmler control of the entire police network. Source 1 shows how it was organised by 1939.

Party control

By 1938 the Nazi Party had five million members and over half a million officials. Its organisation allowed it to supervise every citizen. Source 2 shows how it worked.

The most important people in that huge organisation were the 400,000 Block Leaders. There was a Block Leader on every street and in every block of flats in every town and city. They snooped on their neighbours and reported suspicious behaviour to their Party bosses. In this way, political opponents and petty criminals could be identified and turned over to the police.

Source 1

How the Nazi police was organised.

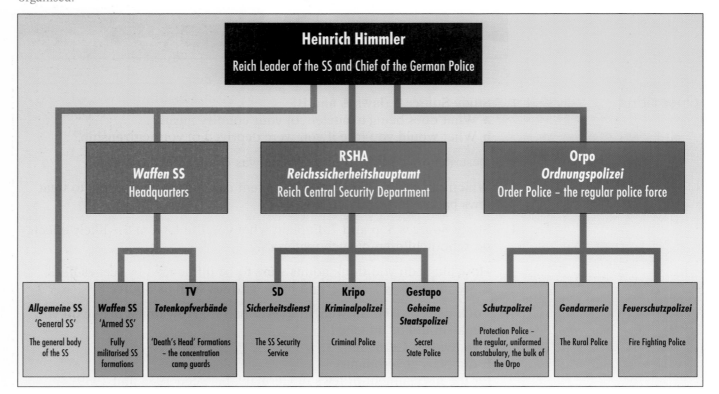

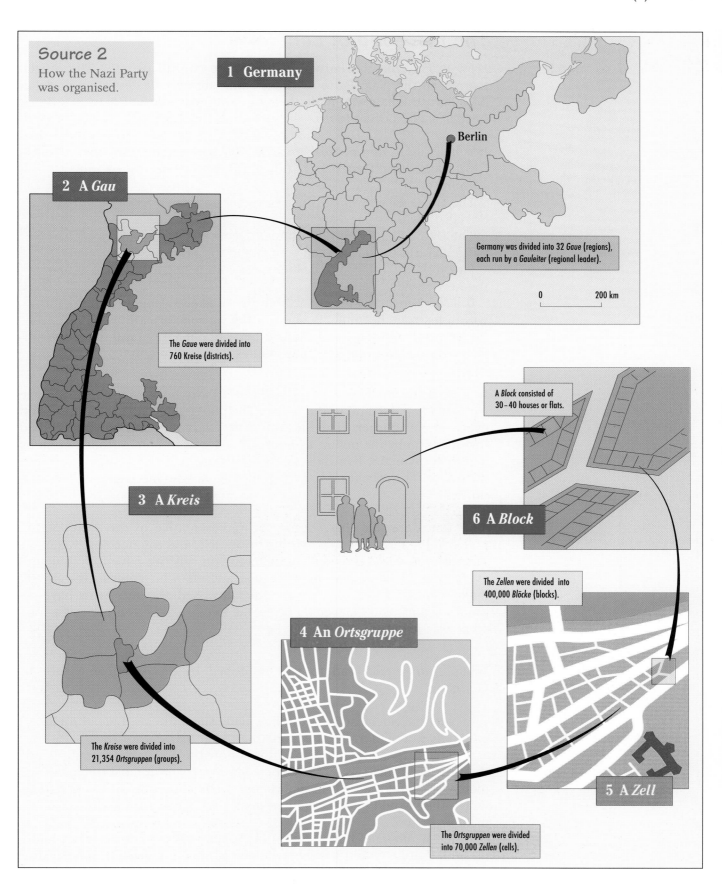

Source 2
How the Nazi Party was organised.

1 Germany

Berlin

Germany was divided into 32 *Gaue* (regions), each run by a *Gauleiter* (regional leader).

0   200 km

2 A *Gau*

The *Gaue* were divided into 760 *Kreise* (districts).

A *Block* consisted of 30–40 houses or flats.

6 A *Block*

3 A *Kreis*

The *Zellen* were divided into 400,000 *Blöcke* (blocks).

The *Kreise* were divided into 21,354 *Ortsgruppen* (groups).

4 An *Ortsgruppe*

5 A *Zell*

The *Ortsgruppen* were divided into 70,000 *Zellen* (cells).

The methods of control

How exactly did the Party and the police control people? The official manual of the Nazi Party provides some answers. It described in detail how Party officials should do their work. Source 3 describes what a Block Leader was expected to do:

Source 3

Organisation Book of the NSDAP, Central Publishing House of the NSDAP, 1943.

It is his duty to find people spreading damaging rumours and to report them to the local leader so that they may be reported to the state authorities.

The Block Leader must…be a preacher and defender of National Socialist ideas.

The Block Leader must continually remind Party members of their particular duties towards the people and the State.

Furthermore, the Block Leader must complete a list (card file) about the households.

It is the Block Leader's aim…that the sons and daughters of families within his zone become members of the various formations of the Hitler Youth, SA, SS…and the German Labour Front, and that they visit National Socialist meetings, rallies, celebrations, etc.

If a Block Leader reported a person to a Party boss, that person's name was usually passed on to the police. The police thus had eyes and ears on every street corner. This meant that everyone and anyone risked investigation by the police, as Source 4 suggests. It comes from a book by a German woman, Eva Lips, about how her husband was denounced to the police. The speaker is a secret police agent who has just searched their house:

Source 4

Eva Lips, *What Hitler Did to Us. A Personal Record of the Third Reich*, 1938.

'Our times are like this', began the representative of the secret state police. 'One must keep everything to oneself, and say nothing. Keep as quiet as possible; keep your thoughts to yourself. We have to follow up every case of denunciation. We…urge anyone who comes near us to make denunciations. Have you any dismissed servants who have a grudge against you? Have you neglected to pay a bill? You can't imagine what *that* leads to.

What *'that'* could lead to was described by an American visitor to Germany:

Source 5

Nora Waln, *Reaching for the Stars*, 1939.

The National Socialist Secret Police made silent arrests. Late at night and early in the morning they took man after man….

As accurately as I could learn, this is how the arrests were made. The door-bell or knocker sounded. There stood two, or at most three, tall men with pairs of pistols in their belts…. The chosen hour was one at which they would find the wanted man relaxed, surprising him at a meal or in bed.

Other members of the household behaved as if hypnotised. They had no faith that he would have any chance of freeing himself by any legal means.... Their minds were filled with memories of what they knew of others who had been taken in this way – disappearing for ever, returned in a closed coffin, or, if let out alive, coming back starved in body and crazed in mind. Yet they did nothing. Family and friends let their man go....

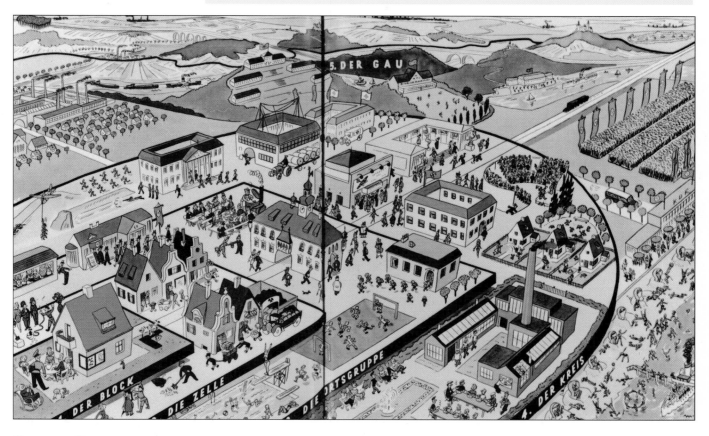

Source 6

A picture from the German propaganda magazine *Signal* in 1941 shows a happy and harmonious people living in 1. *Der Block* – the block, 2. *Die Zelle* – the cell, 3. *Die Ortsgruppe* – the locality, 4. *Der Kreis* – the area, and 5. *Der Gau* – the region.

Questions

1 Many Germans called Block Leaders 'Little Hitlers' behind their backs. Judging by Source 3, why do you think they did so?

2 Source 5 says that few families did anything to stop their menfolk being arrested:
   a Suggest ways in which they could have tried to help their menfolk.
   b Why do you think they did nothing?

3 a Describe the Nazi Party's control of Germany as it appears in Source 6.
   b What is there in Sources 3–5 to suggest that Source 6 was a very one-sided view of how the Nazis controlled Germany?

Rearmament and the economy

Hitler aimed to make Germany powerful. This meant building up its armed forces. In other words, he aimed to rearm Germany.

Rearmament

In 1934, a year after seizing power, Hitler ordered an increase in the armed forces. The army was to grow from 100,000 to 300,000 men. The navy was to build submarines and two battleships. An air force was to be created.

This was forbidden by the Treaty of Versailles. If the Allies found out what was happening, there was a risk that they would invade Germany to stop it. So the armed forces expanded in secret. Air force pilots trained secretly in flying clubs. Bombers were disguised as airliners.

In 1935 Hitler felt strong enough to start rearming openly. He announced that all men would have to do military service when they reached 18, and that the army would grow to 550,000 men. As Hitler had calculated, the Allies protested but did nothing to stop him.

The Four Year Plan

Rearmament was very expensive, but Germany had not yet recovered from the Depression. Germany could not afford such large armed forces.

Hitler's answer to this problem was to introduce a Four Year Plan in 1935 for developing the German economy. One of its chief aims was to make the country self-sufficient in food and raw materials. This would save money by cutting the amount of goods bought from other countries. Artificial substitutes were therefore developed for materials imported from overseas. Textiles were made from pulped wood, rubber from coal and lime, coffee from acorns, petrol from coal, and so on.

There were no substitutes for some things, so Germans ran short of some basic foods and goods. Animal fats such as butter were in particularly short supply. However, the man in charge of the Four Year Plan, Hermann Goering, said in a speech in 1936: 'Would you rather have butter or guns? Shall we bring in lard or iron ore? I tell you, guns make us powerful. Butter only makes us fat.'

Guns or butter?

Given the choice between 'guns and butter', what did Germans prefer? Source 1 provides one answer. In it, an American journalist living in Germany describes what happened when Hitler announced that young men would have to do military service.

Source 1

William Shirer, *Berlin Diary. The Journal of a Foreign Correspondent, 1934–1941*, 1941.

A big crowd gathered...in front of the Chancellery this evening and cheered Hitler until he appeared at a window and saluted. Today's creation of a conscript army in defiance of the Versailles Treaty will greatly enhance his position, for there are few Germans...who will not support it wholeheartedly. The great majority will like the way he has thumbed his nose at Versailles....

Source 2

This picture by John Heartfield appeared in the banned Communist magazine AIZ ('Workers' Illustrated Paper') in December 1935. The caption says 'Hurrah, the butter is all gone.'

Not every German welcomed guns rather than butter. The artist John Heartfield made fun of Goering's 'guns or butter' speech with the picture shown in Source 2.

But was John Heartfield right? Did food run as short as his picture suggested? The figures in Source 3 show that the answer is not quite so simple.

Hurrah, die Butter ist alle!

Goering in seiner Hamburger Rede: „Erz hat stets ein Reich stark gemacht Butter und Schmalz haben höchstens ein Volk fett gemacht'

Source 3

Otto Nathan, *The Nazi Economic System. Germany's Mobilisation for War*, 1944.

Consumption by working-class families in 1927 and 1937

	1927	1937
Rye bread (kg)	262.9	316.1
Fish (kg)	21.8	20.4
White bread (kg)	55.2	30.8
Vegetables (kg)	117.2	109.6
Beef and veal (kg)	21.6	21.4
Potatoes (kg)	499.5	519.8
Other meats (kg)	133.7	109.2
Sugar (kg)	47.2	45.0
Bacon (kg)	9.5	8.5
Tropical fruit (kg)	9.7	6.1
Butter (kg)	15.7	18.0
Coffee (kg)	3.3	3.8
Milk (litres)	427.8	367.2
Beer (litres)	76.5	31.6
Cheese (kg)	13.0	14.5
Cigarettes (number)	450	503
Eggs (number)	404	237

Questions

1   According to Source 1, what did many Germans feel about the start of compulsory military service?

2   Study Source 3 carefully.
   a Which items were people consuming (i) more of (ii) less of in 1937 than in 1927?
   b Does Source 3 suggest that Germans had to eat less because of the Nazi 'guns or butter' policy? Explain your answer.

3   **a** Study Source 2. What do you think John Heartfield wanted people to think when they saw this picture?
   b How do Sources 1 and 3 together suggest that rearmament was not as unpopular as critics like John Heartfield claimed?

Unit 6 Review

Source 1 is taken from a conversation in 1980 between two 60-year-old Germans. The first was a writer, Bernt Engelmann, the other was his old school friend:

Source 1

Bernt Engelmann, *In Hitler's Germany. Everyday Life in the Third Reich*, 1988.

The elimination of unemployment must have made quite an impression on the workers, since they were the ones most affected?

People let themselves be dazzled by that. It was the Nazis' main argument. Today we know for a fact what we only suspected back then: not until the autumn of 1936 was unemployment reduced to anything near a normal level. So it took almost four years, and during the same time, the other major industrialised countries had recovered from the Depression without resorting to terror, or drastic measures, or the massive war preparations that Germany used for getting the unemployed off the streets.

Source 2

Percentage of the workforce unemployed in Germany, the UK and USA, 1925–39.

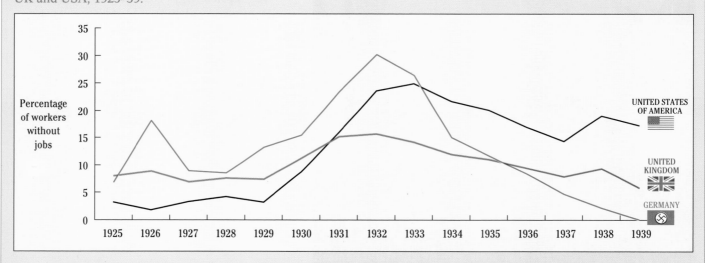

Questions

1   Which of the following statements made in Source 1 can be confirmed by the information in Source 2?
   a 'not until the autumn of 1936 was unemployment reduced to anything near a normal level'.
   b 'during the same time, the other major industrialised countries had recovered from the Depression'.

2   Using the information in Unit 6 of this book give examples of what the speaker in Source 1 might have meant by:
   a terror
   b drastic measures
   c massive war preparations that Germany 'used for getting the unemployed off the streets'.

3   In the light of your answers to questions 1 and 2, explain why you agree or disagree with the views expressed in Source 1.

Unit 7 · The totalitarian state: life in Nazi Germany (2)

This painting by a Nazi artist, Richard Spitz, is called *Nazi Vision of Greatness*. It shows Stormtroopers and workers, men and women, young and old, as well as the spirits of the dead, all under the control of the Nazi Party. In the foreground a Stormtrooper collapses in ecstasy on seeing this vision.

One of the Nazi leaders, Robert Ley, said in 1937 that 'the only people who have a private life in Germany today are those who are asleep'. What was it like to live in a country like that? This unit tries to answer that question by showing how the Nazis controlled women, young people and churchgoers. So total was their control that Germany has often been described as a 'totalitarian state'.

Women

German women in the 1920s had several rights and freedoms which most other women did not have. They had the right to vote. Women working for the government got the same pay as men. Many entered the law and medicine on the same footing as men. Under Nazi rule, however, they lost these gains. They were forced back into traditional roles as wives and mothers. Why did the Nazis do this?

Why did the Nazis restrict women's lives?

In Nazi eyes, a woman's most important function was to bear children, preferably boys. Germany's birth-rate was sinking fast, so the Nazis needed to reverse that in order to provide the army with more soldiers. They introduced measures to increase the birth-rate as soon as they came to power. One such measure was a system of 'marriage loans':

Source 1

From the Law for the Reduction of Unemployment, 1 June 1933

* **1,000 marks** The average wage in 1933 was 150 marks a month. A loan was therefore worth just over half a year's earnings.

> People of German nationality who marry...can be granted a marriage loan of up to 1,000 Reichsmarks*.... The conditions are as follows:
> **a** That the future wife has spent at least six months in employment....
> **b** That the future wife gives up her job....
> **c** That the future wife promises not to take up employment so long as her future husband earns more than 125 Reichsmarks a month.

If a couple took a loan and then had a baby, the repayment of the loan was cut by a quarter. On the birth of a second child, the repayment was cut by a half. After four children they owed nothing.

The marriage loan system encouraged many young people to marry early. As a result, the number of marriages rose from half a million in 1932 to three-quarters of a million in 1934. It did not, however, result in more babies. Most couples continued to have families of two children.

The government tried other schemes to increase the birth-rate. It increased maternity benefits. It introduced family allowances. And it gave medals to the most fertile mothers each year: bronze for those with five children, silver for six or seven, and gold for eight or more.

Underlying all these schemes were Nazi ideas about family life. Sources 2 and 3 reflect some of those ideas.

Source 2

From a pamphlet published by the Nazi Party and sent to many young German women.

* **spouse** A husband or wife.

> 1 Remember that you are a German!
> 2 If you are genetically healthy, do not stay single!
> 3 Keep your body pure!
> 4 Keep your mind and spirit pure!
> 5 Marry only for love!
> 6 As a German, choose only a spouse* of similar or related blood!
> 7 In choosing a spouse, ask about his forebears!
> 8 Health is essential to physical beauty!
> 9 Don't look for a playmate but for a companion in marriage!
> 10 You should want to have as many children as possible!

Source 3

A poster issued in 1937 says 'The NSDAP [Nazi Party] protects the national community' and 'National comrades. If you need help or advice, turn to your local Party organisation.'

Not every woman was encouraged to have babies. A 'Law for the Prevention of Hereditarily Diseased Offspring' ordered that women 'unfit' to be mothers must be sterilised. By 1937 almost 100,000 women had been sterilised. Source 4 reveals the kind of women classed as 'unfit'. It was written by an American teacher living in Berlin who was taken on a tour of the city's schools and children's facilities.

Source 4

Gregor Ziemer, *Education for Death*, 1941.

'Here is the place where we prove that our interest in the child begins before he is born. This is the *Frauen-Klinik* – a city hospital for women'.

We climbed some stairs and entered a second floor gallery, separated from an…operating room by a glass wall. Down below six doctors were hard at work.

What I saw drove the blood from my face…. Hospital beds came and went with methodical precision. The doctors made quick, deft incisions in white abdomen walls:.

'What are they doing?' I asked.

'…These doctors', he said, 'are sterilising women….'

I asked what type of women…and was informed they were the mentally sick, women with low resistance, women who had proved through other births that their offspring were not strong….

'We are even eradicating colour-blindness…' my SS guide told me. 'We must not have soldiers who are colour blind. It is transmitted only by women.'

Source 5

Girls at school are taught how to make a meal for four people.

Bringing women into line

Like every other group in Germany, women's groups were 'brought into line' after 1933. They were all merged into a single 'German Women's Enterprise', the *Deutsches Frauenwerk*. This organisation had at least six million members. It organised Mothers' Schools to train women in household and parenting skills. It organised courses, lectures and radio programmes on household topics.

But this was not the only way in which women were brought into line. Shortly after the Nazi seizure of power, thousands of married women doctors and civil servants were sacked from their jobs. Over the next few years, the number of women

teachers was gradually reduced. From 1936 onwards women could no longer be judges or prosecutors, nor could they serve on juries.

Instead of going out to work, women were asked to stick to the 'three Ks' – *Kinder, Kirche* und *Küche*, which means 'children, church and kitchen'. Source 5 shows girls at school being taught about the third of the three Ks. But when war came in 1939, women were also encouraged to support the war effort. Source 6 reflects this change of policy.

The Nazi Party even ran campaigns to change the way women dressed and looked. Make-up and trousers were discouraged. Hair was to be worn in plaits or a bun, but not dyed or permed. Slimming was frowned upon because being slim was considered bad for child-bearing. Source 3 is an example of the look favoured by the Nazis.

Source 6

A propaganda poster of 1944 encouraging women to support the war effort by working in factories and hospitals and on farms.

Questions

1 Study Source 1 and the paragraph which follows it.
   a How much could newly-wed couples borrow from the government?
   b How many weeks would they need to work to earn the same as this?
   c How could couples avoid repaying all or part of the loan?
   d How do your answers to **a**, **b** and **c** help to explain why the number of marriages rose from 500,000 to 750,000 in the year after marriage loans were introduced?

2 Look at sections a, b, and c of Source 1. What purpose, other than encouraging couples to have babies, did this law seem to have?

3 Study Sources 2 and 4.
   a What kinds of children did the Nazis want women to bear?
   b Find at least two ways in which they tried to ensure that women had only such children.

4 Using all the sources and information in this section, explain (a) how, and (b) why Nazis restricted the lives of women.

5 What change in Nazi views about women can be seen in Source 6? Suggest a reason for this change.

Young people

Nazi schools

Until 1933 most schools in Germany were run by the local state governments. After the Nazis took power, control of the schools was taken from the states and given to a Ministry of Education in Berlin. Many changes followed from this. Jewish teachers were sacked. All other teachers had to take an oath of loyalty to Hitler and join a Nazi Teachers' League. Textbooks were rewritten to include Nazi ideas. Courses in German history, politics and 'racial hygiene' were introduced. Religious education was scrapped. The number of PE classes was doubled.

The youth movement

Outside school, the Nazi Party took control of Germany's many youth groups. A law of 1936 merged all youth groups into the 'Hitler Youth Movement'. Two further laws in 1939 made membership compulsory. Source 1 shows the four main groups in the Hitler Youth. Sources 2 and 3 give an idea of what these groups were like.

Young rebels

By 1940, as Source 1 shows, nearly every youngster belonged to the Hitler Youth. But some avoided becoming members and formed their own groups. The largest of these rebel groups was the Edelweiss Pirates. They listened to forbidden Swing music, danced the forbidden Jitterbug, wore tartan clothes, and grew their hair in long side-locks. They alarmed the authorities with 'anti-social' behaviour such as writing anti-Nazi graffiti on walls and picking fights with the Hitler Youth.

Source 1

Membership and structure of the Hitler Youth Movement, 1934–40.

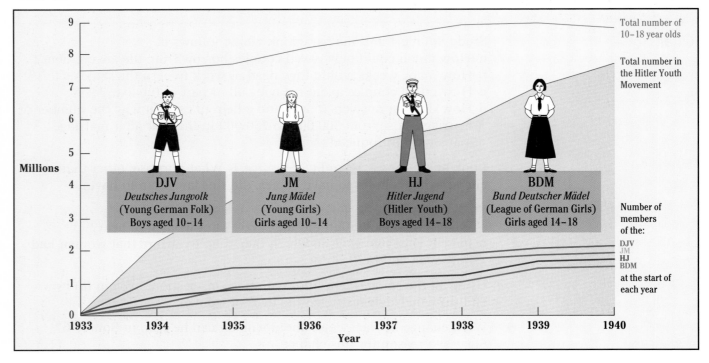

The Hitler Youth: for and against

Source 2

Boys of the DJV (Young German Folk) parade for a tent inspection in their camp at Tempelhof Field, Berlin, in June 1934.

What was the Hitler Youth Movement like? What did youngsters get from it, and why did some rebel against it? One answer can be found in the Movement's rule book, from which Source 3 is taken. It describes what boys of 10-14 had to do to get a 'Badge of Achievement'.

Source 3

Pimpf in Dienst ('Boys in the Service'), 1937.

* **Indoctrination** Teaching ideas to young people in such a way that they accept them without question as true.

The following are the conditions for bestowal of the badge:

(1) Indoctrination*
1 Life of the Führer
2 Germans abroad
3 Lost territories
4 Holidays of the German people
5 Five flag oaths
6 Six Hitler Youth Songs:
  a Brothers in Pits and Mines
  b Grey Heaven
  c Holy Fatherland....

(2) Athletic achievements
1 Running, 60 metres – 10 seconds
2 Long jump – 3.25 metres
3 Ball throwing – 35 metres
4 Pull up on the bar – twice
5 Somersaults...twice backwards
6 Swimming 100 metres
7 Ability to ride a bicycle

(3) Hiking and camping
1 A day's hike of 15 kilometres with a light pack (not over 5 kg)....
2 Participation in a camp, living in tents for at least three days.
3 Put up a pup tent and help put up a barge tent.
4 Construct a cooking pit; fetch water for cooking.
5 Know the names of the most important trees.
6 Orient a map from the stars.
7 Know the most important symbols on a 1:25,000 map....

(4) Target practice
Shooting with an air gun, distance 8 metres in sitting position. A bull's eye with twelve concentric circles; distance of circles 0.5 cm.

What did members of the Hitler Youth think about these camps? A member of the BDM, Melita Maschmann, later wrote this about a BDM camp:

Source 4

From the autobiography of Melita Maschmann, translated into English as *Account Rendered. A Dossier on my Former Self*, 1964.

Our camp community was a reduced model of that which I imagined our national community to be. It was a completely successful model. Never before or since have I had the experience of such a good community.... Among us were peasant girls, students, workers, shop assistants, hairdressers, pupils, clerks and so on.

Source 5

The title page of *Kamaradschaft* ('Comradeship'), an illegal, underground youth magazine of 1938.

As Source 1 shows, nearly a million young people had still not joined the Hitler Youth Movement in 1940, even though it was meant to be compulsory. The feelings of some of those rebels can be guessed at from Source 5.

The Nazi authorities took a dim view of young people who formed their own groups, as Source 6 suggests. It is a report sent to the Gestapo by the Nazi Party in Düsseldorf.

Source 6

Hauptstaatsarchiv Düsseldorf (Düsseldorf State Archives)

Re: Edelweiss Pirates question.... These youngsters, aged between 12 and 17, hang around into the late evening, with musical instruments and young females. Since this riff-raff is to a large extent outside the Hitler Youth and adopts a hostile attitude towards it, they are a danger to other young people.... There is a suspicion that it is these youths who have been inscribing the walls of the subway on the *Altenbergstrasse* with the slogans 'Down with Hitler'...'Down with Nazi brutality' etc.

Questions

1 Read Source 3 carefully. What does it tell you about
  a what young people did in the Hitler Youth
  b the aims of the Hitler Youth Movement?

2 **a** Study Source 2. What do you think were the attractions of this camp?
  b What else was good about Hitler Youth camps according to Source 4?

3 Source 1 shows that seven million young people joined the Hitler Youth before membership was made compulsory in 1939. Does this prove that most young Germans liked the movement? Explain your answer.

4 Look at Sources 5 and 6. What do they tell you about why some young people did not join the Hitler Youth?

5 **a** What were the likely consequences of being reported to the Gestapo?
  b Why, despite the risk of these consequences, do you think the Edelweiss Pirates risked doing the things described in Source 6?

Christianity and the Nazis

The programme of the Nazi Party said that they believed in 'positive Christianity'. It spoke of 'freedom for all religious denominations'. Yet within months of seizing power, the Nazis were doing their best to damage the Christian faith.

The Catholic Church

In 1933 Hitler signed a Concordat, or agreement, with the Pope. It said that the Nazis would not interfere in the Catholic Church. In return, the Pope ordered bishops to take an oath of loyalty to Hitler.

Hitler had no intention of keeping this agreement. Church schools were shut down. The Catholic Youth League was broken up. Many monasteries were closed.

The Pope protested in 1937 by issuing an encyclical. This was a letter to be read out in all Catholic churches in Germany. It condemned the Nazis for being 'hostile to Christ and his Church'. But it had no effect. The Nazis not only continued to attack the Church but also started to arrest priests and put them into concentration camps.

The Protestant Churches

Germany's Protestants belonged to 28 church groups. In 1933, under Nazi pressure, they agreed to unite to form a 'Reich Church'. They elected a Nazi as their 'Reich Bishop' and expelled 'non-Aryan' pastors.

The keenest members of the Reich Church called themselves 'German Christians'. They wore Nazi uniforms and gave the German greeting. Their slogan was 'The swastika on our chests and the Cross in our hearts'.

Many Protestants hated this. A group of pastors led by Martin Niemöller broke away from the Reich Church and set up their own 'Confessional Church'. More than 6,000 pastors joined it, leaving only

Source 1

German Christian students holding an open-air religious meeting in Berlin in 1938.

2,000 in the Reich Church. This was a clear challenge to Nazi power. As a result some 800 pastors were arrested. Many, including Niemöller, were put in concentration camps.

Religious sects

Some religious sects refused all co-operation with the Nazis. Jehovah's Witnesses, for example, followed the teaching of the Bible not to take up weapons in any cause. So they refused to serve in the army or to have anything to do with the Nazis. In retaliation, the SS imprisoned whole families of Jehovah's Witnesses. About a third of all Jehovah's Witnesses were murdered in concentration camps.

Many other sects and groups were also suppressed. The Salvation Army, Christian Scientists and Seventh Day Adventists all disappeared. Even astrologers, faith healers and fortune tellers were banned.

Pagan cults

Many non-Christian sects sprang up to replace the sects which were suppressed. Chief among them was the German Faith Movement. All were pro-Nazi and all were racist. Most were pagan cults which worshipped the sun and the seasons instead of the Christian God.

How Christian were the Nazis?

The Nazis said they believed in 'positive Christianity', yet they persecuted Christians of all kinds. So what did they believe? Sources 2–6 illustrate some of the ways in which Nazis practised religion.

Source 2

A prayer which children in Nazi-run orphanages said before meals. Quoted in K. Immer, *Entchristung der Jugend* ('The Dechristianisation of Children'), 1936.

> O Führer, my Führer, sent to me by God,
> Protect and maintain my life.
> Thou hast served Germany in its hour of need.
> I now thank thee for my daily bread.
> Oh! Stay with me, Oh! Never leave me,
> Führer, My Führer, my faith and life.

Source 3

An evening prayer said in a Catholic girls' school in Breslau in 1934. Quoted in Klaus Scholder, *The Churches and the Third Reich*, 1988.

> Dear God in heaven above,
> send angels with your love,
> to stand around my bed
> when I lay down my head.
>
> Your fairest angel there,
> with bright and radiant hair,
> in radiant silver gown
> send to our Hitler down.
>
> May He protect his sleep,
> him from all danger keep,
> that next day he may wake
> for our dear country's sake.

Source 4

A song printed in *Neues Lieder der Hitler Jugend* (*New Songs of the Hitler Youth*), no date.

> We are the merry Hitler Youth,
> we need none of your Christian truth,
> for Adolf Hitler is our Leader,
> our redeemer and our feeder.
>
> No pope, no villain, bars our way,
> we Hitler Youth will have our say.
> Horst Wessel* leads us, Christ is nix*.
> Who wants incense and crucifix?
>
> We do not need the church to bless,
> the swastika brings us happiness....

* **Horst Wessel** A Nazi Stormtrooper killed in a street battle with Communists in 1932, and later elevated into a Nazi hero.
* **nix** Nothing.

Source 5

A sermon preached at Christmas in 1936 by a member of the German Faith Movement, quoted in J.S.Conway, *The Nazi Persecution of the Churches*, 1968.

Christmas is the feast of light of our ancestors, the ancient Germans, and so is several thousand years old. In the height of the winter solstice between 23–25 of the Yule month, the various members of each family...met under a tree in the woods. The Winter Man, old Ruprecht, … appeared and gave out gifts. Burning torches were attached to a tree and soon the...darkness was lit by the burning flames of the Christmas tree…. Having sung some Xmas songs, our fore-fathers went home with the knowledge and joy in their hearts that...they were not forgotten or forsaken by their God. From now on the sun rose higher day after day....

And just as our ancestors did not lose their faith in the coming light...so we too stand today in the light after long darkness. Germany, after the Great War, was threatened with collapse. But then...happened that greatest miracle: Germany awoke and followed the sign of light, the swastika.

Source 6

Women dressed in Bronze Age costumes take part in a harvest festival in 1933.

Questions

Work in a group of five.

1 Each choose one of Sources 2–6. Study your source, then make a note of:
   a anything that shows a belief in the Christian God.
   b anything that shows lack of belief, or disbelief, in the Christian God.
   c anything that shows a non-Christian belief.
   d anything that is similar to a Christian belief without being Christian.

2 Use your notes to prepare a one-minute talk for the rest of your group, or for the class, explaining what it tells you about Nazi views of Christianity.

Propaganda and 'thought control'

People in Nazi Germany could not talk, write or even think freely. A Department of Public Propaganda and Enlightenment had the job of controlling their opinions and beliefs. It was led by Doctor Joseph Goebbels.

The press

Goebbels used every known technique of propaganda. First, he made sure that the press put across Nazi views. Non-Nazi newspapers were taken over by a Nazi publishing company until two-thirds of the press were under its control. Newspaper editors were told each day what news they could or could not print.

Radio

Next, all radio stations were brought under Nazi control, allowing Goebbels to broadcast Nazi ideas. Mass-produced radios called 'the People's Receiver' were sold so cheaply that seven out of ten homes had one by 1939. To make sure that people could listen to the radio when not at home, workplaces, cafés and other public places had to turn on their radios for important programmes. From 1938, loud-speakers were put up on posts in many city streets.

Rallies and campaigns

Third, Goebbels used rallies and campaigns to increase people's loyalty to the Party. Each year a mass rally at Nuremberg brought together hundreds of thousands of people for spectacular parades and displays in four huge arenas (see page 72). In between rallies, local SA or Hitler Youth groups campaigned to raise funds for the Party. The most frequent campaigns were for 'one-pot Sundays', when families were expected to cook Sunday lunch in a single pot and give the money saved to collectors when they called in the afternoon.

Source 1

This poster was published by the Ministry of Public Propaganda and Enlightenment, encouraging people to buy the People's Receiver radio (*Volksempfänger*). It says, 'All Germany can hear the Führer with the People's Receiver'.

Ganz Deutschland hört den Führer
mit dem Volksempfänger

Source 2
Students and Stormtroopers burning books written by Jews and Communists in Berlin in May 1933.

Misinformation

Propaganda sometimes took the form of lies. 'Whisper propaganda', for example, involved planting false rumours and spreading false information by chain letters, while children's schoolbooks were rewritten to include Nazi ideas.

Restrictions on free expression

As well as propaganda, Goebbels used censorship to control people's thoughts. Books were the first form of expression to be censored. Encouraged by Goebbels, students in Berlin burnt 20,000 books written by Jews and Communists in a massive bonfire in 1933. Libraries took forbidden books off their shelves. Bookshops were raided.

Entertainment and culture were censored. Jazz music and the 'jitterbug' dance were banned because black people had originated them. Much modern art was condemned as 'degenerate' and thrown out of art galleries. Films and plays were vetted for nudity and sex scenes.

Censorship even went as far as private conversations. A 'Law Against Malicious Gossip' in 1934 forbade the telling of anti-Nazi jokes and stories. The penalties for being caught doing so were fines and prison.

What made Nazi thought control so effective?

With the press, radio, cinema, theatre and books all under Nazi control, most Germans were affected in some way by Nazi ideas. What made Goebbels so good at his job? Why was his propaganda so effective?

Goebbels' success was partly due to his ability to put out propaganda on a national scale. This can be seen in Sources 3 and 4. Source 3 is an announcement which appeared in a local newspaper in 1934.

Source 3

From the local newspaper in Neu-Isenberg, near Frankfurt, on 16 March 1934. Quoted in J.Noakes and G.Pridham (eds), *Nazism 1919–1945*, 1984.

Attention! The Führer is speaking on the radio. On Wednesday 21 March the Führer is speaking on all German stations from 11.00 to 11.50 a.m. ...The district Party headquarters has ordered that all factory owners, department stores, offices, shops, pubs and blocks of flats put up loudspeakers an hour before the broadcast...so that the whole work force and all national comrades can participate....

Source 4

A painting by Paul Mathias Padua, *The Führer Speaks* (1937), shows an entire family listening to a radio broadcast by Hitler. This was the kind of art favoured by the Nazi authorities.

But Goebbels used propaganda on a local as well as a national scale, as Source 5 shows. It is taken from an interview recorded in 1970 by an American historian with one of Goebbels' assistants:

Source 5

Doctor Leopold Gutterer, State Secretary at the Ministry of Propaganda, interviewed by Jay W.Baird in *The Mythical World of Nazi War Propaganda 1939-1945*, 1974.

* **Berlin-Wedding** A working class area of Berlin which was strongly pro-Communist and anti-Nazi.
* **Dachau** A concentration camp.

Goebbels was very clever at propaganda...when special occasions arose. One remarkable example occurred on Christmas Eve, 1933, in communist Berlin-Wedding*. There...the Ministry gathered together the families of most of the Communists who had been incarcerated in Dachau*. Party officials passed out candy, toys and clothing to the wives and children, while an SA band provided sentimental Christmas carols as background music. At the correct psychological moment, as the band struck up 'Old Comrades', SS vans rolled up and unloaded a large group of prisoners, who were delivered to their families as free men as a 'Christmas gift from the Führer'.

Source 6

This poster says, 'This hand leads the Reich. Young Germans follow it in the ranks of the HJ (Hitler Youth)'.

Children and young people were particular targets of Nazi propaganda. As well as in posters like Source 6, Nazi ideas could be put into the things they read. Source 7 is an example of the kind of material published in school textbooks after 1933.

Source 7

Quoted in J.Noakes and G.Pridham (eds), *Nazism 1919–1945. A Documentary Reader*, 1984.

Question 97. To keep a mentally ill person costs approx 4 Reichsmarks per day, a cripple 5.50 RM, a criminal 3.50. Many civil servants receive only 4 RM per day, white collar employees barely 3.50 RM, unskilled workers not even 2 RM for their families.

a Illustrate these figures with a diagram. (According to conservative estimates there are 300,000 mentally ill etc in care.)
b How much do these people cost to keep in total, at a cost of 4 RM per head?
c How many marriage loans at 1,000 RM each...could be granted from this money?

Questions

1   **a** Find three forms of propaganda in the painting in Source 4.
    b Why might this painting itself be described as propaganda?

2   Study Source 5. How likely was this, do you think, to change the way people in that area thought about the Nazis? Explain your answer.

3   Study Source 7.
    a What do you think were the purposes of this mathematics exercise?
    b What effects do you think it might have had on schoolchildren who did the exercise?

4   Look at the poster in Source 6.
    a What effect do you think the artist wanted the poster to have on people?
    b What methods did the artist use to make the poster effective?

5   Sources 1–7 in this section show seven different ways of trying to control people's thoughts. Choose the three which you think were most likely to have this effect. Explain your choices.

Unit 7 Review

Despite all the restrictions on what they did and said, people still told jokes about Hitler and the Nazis. But sometimes snooping neighbours reported the jokers to the authorities. Each of the following question-and-answer jokes (a favourite form of joke in the 1930s) resulted in the joker going to prison. Read them and then answer the questions beneath.

Source 1

David Welch, *Propaganda and the German Cinema*, 1983.

* **tall like Hitler...** Hitler was of average height, Goebbels had dark hair, and Goering was fat.

> *Question:* What is an Aryan?
> *Answer:* An Aryan is a man who is tall like Hitler, blonde like Goebbels and slim like Goering*.

Source 2

William Shirer, *Berlin Diary*, 1941.

> *Question:* An aeroplane carrying Hitler, Goering and Goebbels crashes. All three are killed. Who is saved?
> *Answer:* The German people.

Source 3

Marlis G.Steinart, *Hitler's War and the Germans*, 1977.

> *Question:* Have you read what it says for butter in the new Meyers dictionary?
> *Answer:* Something spread on bread in the days of the Weimar Republic.

Questions

1 **a** The first two jokes are about Hitler, Goebbels and Goering. What posts did they have in the government?
  b Source 2 suggests that the Germans would have been better off if Hitler, Goebbels and Goering were killed in a plane crash. For each of the three men, give examples of what they had done to make people feel like this.

2 Source 1 refers to Aryans.
  a What does the term 'Aryan' mean?
  b How does this joke suggest that some Germans were not convinced by Nazi ideas about race?

3 Source 3 suggests that butter was something unknown since the days of the Weimar Republic. Using pages 86–87 for information, explain why people might have thought this.

4 The people who told these jokes were sent to prison for doing so. Why do you think the Nazi authorities thought it was necessary to do so?

Unit 8 · Dictatorship destroyed: Nazi aggression and war, 1935–45

Hitler had three aims in his dealings with other countries. The first was to get back the land taken from Germany in 1919. The second was to unite all German-speaking people in one country. The third was to get extra land for Germany.

Hitler pursued these aims first by rearming Germany and then by taking land from neighbouring countries. This led to war in 1939 when Britain and France tried to stop him. In the world war which followed, Germany expanded to become the largest and strongest country in Europe, before being defeated in 1945.

This unit shows how Germany expanded, and looks at the ways in which Germans, as well as the people they conquered, were affected by six years of world war.

This propaganda poster of 1944 announced that 17-year-olds were to be called up for service in the armed forces. It shows members of the Hitler Youth marching to war, backed by a Panzer tank.

Expansion and aggression 1935–39

Source 1

This poster from a Nazi exhibition shows Germans in national costumes from the lands surrounding Germany. The words say, 'Those from the old German Empire return home.'

The Saar plebiscite, 1935

Hitler's expansion of Germany began democratically, and without aggression, in the Saarland. The Saar was one of Germany's most important coal-producing areas. In 1919 the Treaty of Versailles had put it under League of Nations control and let the French run its coal-mines. After fifteen years, its people could choose between staying under League control, returning to Germany or becoming French. In 1935, when the League held the vote, or 'plebiscite', nine out of ten Saarlanders voted to belong to Germany and so the area was returned to German control.

The remilitarisation of the Rhineland

The Versailles Treaty made the Rhineland a demilitarised zone. This meant that the German army was not allowed within 50 kilometres of the River Rhine. The Locarno Treaties of 1926 confirmed this (see page 45).

Many Germans hated the demilitarised zone. It hurt their national pride and it left their country open to attack. In 1936 Hitler therefore sent 32,000 troops into the Rhineland in order to *re*militarise it.

There was a risk that this would lead to war. The Locarno Treaties said that the Allies could use force to stop German troops entering the Rhineland. However, the French were going through a political crisis at the time. The British felt that Germany was simply 'entering its own back garden'. Neither wanted to go to war over the Rhineland.

Union with Austria, 1938

Hitler's next aim was to unite Germany with Austria. Because this was forbidden by the Versailles Treaty, he had to proceed with great care. He began by ordering the Austrian Nazi Party to make trouble by staging violent demonstrations and letting off bombs. His aim was to make it look as if the Austrian government could not control the country.

As Hitler intended, the Austrian police could not halt the violence, so Hitler said he would send the German army into Austria to 'restore order'. The Austrian leader protested and made every effort to defend his country against this threat. None of his efforts worked, and he resigned. An Austrian Nazi took his place and immediately asked Hitler to send troops into Austria to restore order.

The German army entered Austria on 12 March 1938. On 13 March, Hitler announced the *Anschluss*, or union, of the two countries in 'Greater Germany'.

The occupation of the Sudetenland, 1938

Hitler used similar methods to get hold of the Sudetenland. This was an area of Czechoslovakia where three million German-speaking people lived. He ordered a Nazi-style party there, the Sudeten People's Party, to make impossible demands for independence which the Czechs were sure to refuse. Then they would stage riots and demonstrations to make it look as if the Czechs could not control the Sudetenland. Hitler would then send the German army to 'restore order'.

Sadly for the Czechs, no other country was willing to help them fight this threat. The British and French, who had the military power to do so, were following a policy of appeasement towards Germany. As a result, they agreed in a conference at Munich that the Czechs should give the Sudetenland to Germany. The area was duly handed over in October 1938.

Source 2

Cheering crowds welcome Hitler into the Sudetenland in October 1938.

Source 3   Six stages in the creation of 'Greater Germany', 1935–39.

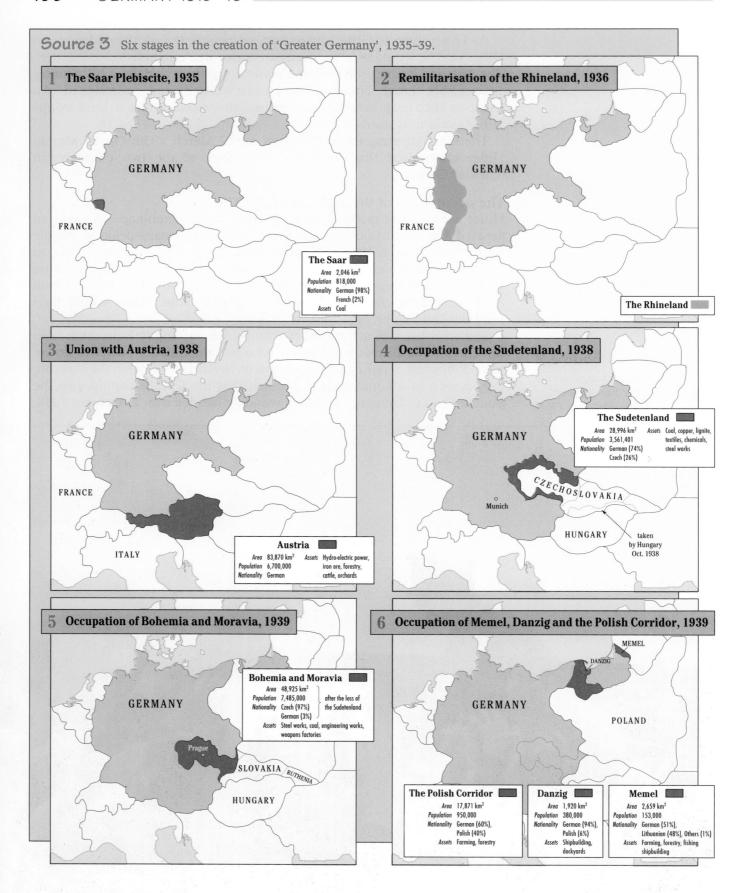

1   The Saar Plebiscite, 1935

GERMANY

FRANCE

The Saar

Area	2,046 km²
Population	818,000
Nationality	German (98%)
	French (2%)
Assets	Coal

2   Remilitarisation of the Rhineland, 1936

GERMANY

FRANCE

The Rhineland

3   Union with Austria, 1938

GERMANY

FRANCE

ITALY

Austria

Area	83,870 km²	Assets	Hydro-electric power,
Population	6,700,000		iron ore, forestry,
Nationality	German		cattle, orchards

4   Occupation of the Sudetenland, 1938

GERMANY

CZECHOSLOVAKIA

Munich

HUNGARY

taken by Hungary Oct. 1938

The Sudetenland

Area	28,996 km²	Assets	Coal, copper, lignite,
Population	3,561,401		textiles, chemicals,
Nationality	German (74%)		steel works
	Czech (26%)		

5   Occupation of Bohemia and Moravia, 1939

GERMANY

Prague

SLOVAKIA   RUTHENIA

HUNGARY

Bohemia and Moravia

Area	48,925 km²	
Population	7,485,000	after the loss of
Nationality	Czech (97%)	the Sudetenland
	German (3%)	
Assets	Steel works, coal, engineering works,	
	weapons factories	

6   Occupation of Memel, Danzig and the Polish Corridor, 1939

MEMEL

DANZIG

GERMANY

POLAND

The Polish Corridor

Area	17,871 km²
Population	950,000
Nationality	German (60%),
	Polish (40%)
Assets	Farming, forestry

Danzig

Area	1,920 km²
Population	380,000
Nationality	German (94%),
	Polish (6%)
Assets	Shipbuilding,
	dockyards

Memel

Area	2,659 km²
Population	153,000
Nationality	German (51%),
	Lithuanian (48%), Others (1%)
Assets	Farming, forestry, fishing
	shipbuilding

The occupation of Bohemia and Moravia, 1939

The Munich Agreement dealt only with the Sudetenland. It said nothing about two million Germans living in the Czech provinces of Bohemia and Moravia. Hitler now aimed to bring them under German control.

Using the same tactics as before, Hitler claimed that the Germans in Bohemia and Moravia were being ill-treated by the Czechs. He said that the Czech government had lost control and that the German army should be sent in to restore control. When Hitler threatened to bomb Prague, the capital, the Czech President gave in to his demands, and invited the German army to occupy the country.

German troops marched into Prague on 15 March 1939. The next day, Bohemia and Moravia became a 'protectorate' of Germany. The province of Slovakia remained independent but had to sign a treaty accepting German protection. The province of Ruthenia was given to Hungary.

Memel

After destroying Czechoslovakia, Hitler turned his attention north. On 23 March 1939 German troops marched into Memel, a German port taken by Lithuania in 1923. They occupied the port and surrounding land, and united it with Germany.

Danzig and the Polish Corridor

The land in the north which Hitler most wanted was the land which divided Germany in two. Germans called it West Prussia and Poles called it the Polish Corridor. Although most people living there were German, the Treaty of Versailles gave it to the Poles so that they could reach the ports on the Baltic Sea. The Treaty also put the German port of Danzig under League of Nations control.

In April 1939 Hitler demanded the return of Danzig as well as a road and a railway across the Polish Corridor. At this point the British and French realised that their policy of appeasement had failed to stop Hitler demanding more land. They dropped the policy and gave the Poles a guarantee to protect them from any German attack.

The Polish guarantee did not scare Hitler. He ordered the army to prepare for an invasion of Poland. To make sure that the Soviet Union did not try to prevent the invasion, he signed a non-aggression pact with the Soviet leaders and agreed to divide Poland between them.

Hitler was convinced that with the Soviet Union neutral, Britain would not risk sending its armies to war with him. Hitler therefore ordered a full-scale invasion of Poland on 1 September 1939.

Questions

1   Look at Source 3.
    a Which areas of land did Germany occupy between 1935 and 1939?
    b In which areas did Hitler act aggressively to get what he wanted?
    c In which areas could Hitler justify his actions by saying he was taking land where mostly Germans lived?
    d What did Germany gain by occupying these areas of land?

2   Compare map 1 with map 6. Describe how Germany in 1939 differed from Germany in 1935.

War and conquest, 1939–42

The fall of Poland

The German invasion of Poland was fast and deadly. Using a new method of warfare known as 'blitzkrieg', or 'lightning war', German armed forces defeated the Polish army in a week. By mid-October 1939 they had occupied half the country.

The war widens

Britain and France declared war on Germany on 3 September. However, it was not until April 1940 that they attacked. The British Royal Navy laid mines in the sea along the coast of Norway to stop iron ore supplies from reaching Germany. The Germans desperately needed iron-ore for making weapons, and could not afford to have their supplies blocked. So, in April 1940, they occupied Norway and Denmark to safeguard the supply route.

The fall of Western Europe

Next, Hitler turned west. On 10 May, using the blitzkrieg method of warfare, the Germans invaded Holland and Belgium, defeating them in three weeks. Then they entered France, defeated the French army and forced the British army to retreat from Dunkirk. On 22 June France surrendered and was divided in two. Northern France was occupied by the Germans. Southern France remained independent but was ruled by a pro-German government in the city of Vichy.

Britain survives

By mid-1940 Hitler's forces controlled a huge area of Europe. His next target was Britain, the only country still at war with him. The German armed forces prepared to invade southern England but were stopped from doing so when the Royal Air Force defeated the German air force in the Battle of Britain in summer 1940. This deprived the invasion fleet of vital air cover, forcing Hitler to cancel the invasion.

War in south-east Europe

Hitler now had to turn his attention to southern Europe where his ally Mussolini, leader of Italy, was in trouble. Mussolini had attacked Greece in October 1940, hoping to get control of the Balkan region. When British forces arrived to help the Greeks in 1941, Hitler decided that he must help Mussolini. He feared that British aircraft in Greece would be able to bomb the oil-fields in Romania from which Germany got much of its oil. So German forces advanced into the Balkan region in spring 1941, occupying both Yugoslavia and Greece.

Invasion of the Soviet Union

In June 1941 Hitler broke the Nazi-Soviet non-aggression pact when he invaded the Soviet Union. The Soviet forces were unprepared for the attack and were forced to retreat deep into the Soviet Union, giving up huge areas to the Germans. By late 1941, Hitler's forces had occupied all of the western Soviet Union and were poised to strike south-east into the valuable oil-fields of the Caucasus.

Questions

Compare the two maps opposite. Then list the ways in which Europe changed under these headings:
a countries which disappeared
b countries which changed
c new countries or regions
d countries occupied by Germany.
e the shape of Germany.

Source 1
The German conquest of Europe, 1939–41.

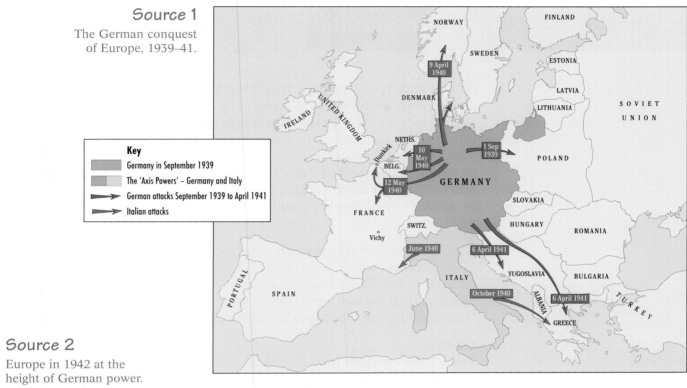

Key
- Germany in September 1939
- The 'Axis Powers' – Germany and Italy
- German attacks September 1939 to April 1941
- Italian attacks

Source 2
Europe in 1942 at the height of German power.

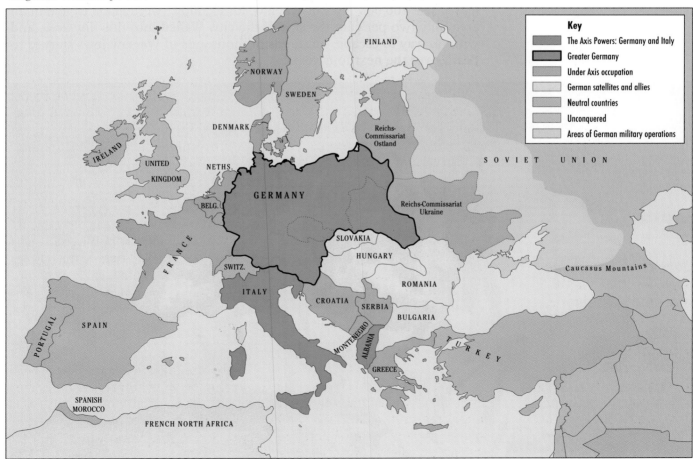

Key
- The Axis Powers: Germany and Italy
- Greater Germany
- Under Axis occupation
- German satellites and allies
- Neutral countries
- Unconquered
- Areas of German military operations

Extermination

As you have read (see page 76), Nazis believed that human beings were divided into races, some 'superior', the rest 'inferior'. In Nazi eyes, the 'Aryan' race was the 'master race' while Jewish people were inferior to all others. They had, therefore, made laws to restrict the activities of Jews. They had taken away German citizenship from them, sacked them from government jobs, and had made them wear yellow stars in public. But this was not enough for the Nazis. In 1939, when the war began, they began to murder Jews and other people whom they called 'undesirables'.

Euthanasia

They took the first step towards mass murder when Hitler ordered the use of euthanasia, which some people call 'mercy killing', for incurably ill patients in hospital. Over the next two years some 70,000 patients were killed by their doctors. After the invasion of Poland, SS troops carried out 'mercy killings' of thousands of patients in Polish mental hospitals.

Ghettos

From 1940 onwards Jews in Poland were made to live in ghettos. These were walled-off areas of towns or cities which they were not allowed to leave. The 400,000 Jews of Warsaw, for example, were made to live in an area only two per cent the size of the city. Walled into this tiny area, and with no way to escape, hundreds of thousands of Warsaw Jews starved to death over the next four years.

Source 1

This photograph, taken by a German soldier, shows a Special Action Group forcing the women and girls of a town called Dvinsk to undress before shooting them.

Source 2

This photograph shows Hungarian Jews, who have just arrived on the train in the background, being divided into two groups: those who were to work as slave labour in the camp, and those who were to be killed in gas chambers.

Special Action Groups

The number of mass murders increased after the invasion of the Soviet Union in July 1941. 'Special Action Groups' of the SS followed the German armies into the Soviet Union. Their orders were to kill the Jews in every captured town and village. They rounded up whole communities of Jews, made them strip naked, and then shot them into mass graves (see Source 1). Some of the Special Action Groups killed Jews by locking them into lorries and pumping in carbon monoxide gas.

The Final Solution

In 1942, when most of Europe was under Nazi rule, the Nazi leaders met at Wannsee, near Berlin, to discuss what they called a 'final solution to the Jewish problem'. At the Wannsee Conference they decided on the murder of every Jew in Europe, either by working them to death or by execution. By 1945, as a result of this decision, some six million Jewish people had been murdered. How was it possible for the Nazis to commit such an appalling crime?

How was such a crime possible?

To kill an estimated 11 million Jews living in Europe, the SS set up five 'extermination camps' in remote areas of Poland. Each of the camps – Belzec, Treblinka, Sobibor, Chelmno, and Auschwitz-Birkenau – was linked by rail to the rest of Europe. Captured Jews were transported to the camps in long trains of goods wagons (see Source 2).

When a train arrived at a death camp, prisoners were taken to what they were told were shower rooms. There they were ordered to undress and to take showers. Sometimes they were given soap and towels. But the shower rooms were, in reality, gas chambers. Source 3 describes what happened in them.

Source 3

From testimony given by a French prisoner in Auschwitz, in the *Trial of the Major War Criminals before the International Military Tribunal*, volume 6, International Military Tribunal, Nuremberg, 1947.

I know these details as I knew a little Jewess from France..., the sole survivor of a family of nine. Her mother and seven brothers and sisters had been gassed on arrival. When I met her she was employed to undress the babies before they were taken into the gas chamber. Once the people were undressed they took them into a room which was somewhat like a shower room, and gas capsules were thrown through an opening in the ceiling. An SS man would watch the effect produced through a porthole. At the end of five or seven minutes, when the gas had completed its work, he gave the signal to open the doors; and men with gas masks – they too were prisoners – went into the room and removed the corpses....

After that a special squad would come to pull out gold teeth and dentures and again, when the bodies had been reduced to ashes, they would sift them in an attempt to recover the gold.

At Auschwitz extermination camp, prisoners were divided into two groups: those who were to die in the gas chambers, and those who were to work (see Source 2). Many of those chosen to work became slave labourers, building a massive factory for making synthetic oil and rubber. Source 4 gives an idea of the conditions in which they lived and worked. Drawn by a teenage prisoner, Ella Liebermann, it shows SS guards taking a roll-call of prisoners, punishing and torturing them in a variety of ways.

Source 4

A drawing by Ella Liebermann, a prisoner in Auschwitz, of roll-call in the camp. The drawing was found by Allied soldiers at the end of the war.

Few prisoners were able to rebel or to escape. Primo Levi, an Italian Jew who survived a year working in Auschwitz, explained why:

Source 5

Primo Levi wrote this as an 'afterword' at the end of his books about the Holocaust, *If This Is A Man* and *The Truce*, in 1987.

* **debilitated** Weakened.

> Escape was difficult and extremely dangerous. The prisoners were debilitated*...by hunger and ill-treatment. Their heads were shaved, their striped clothing was immediately recognisable, and their wooden clogs made silent and rapid walking impossible. They had no money and, in general, did not speak Polish, which was the local language, nor did they have any contacts in the area. On top of that, fierce reprisals were employed to discourage escape attempts. Anyone caught trying to escape was publicly hanged – often after cruel torture.

Although few Jews were able to escape from the camps, or to rebel against their guards, Jews in the ghettos organised resistance on a number of occasions. Their greatest act of resistance took place in the Warsaw Ghetto in April 1943. On 19 April thousands of German troops entered the ghetto to remove all remaining Jews to the extermination camps. Several hundred Jews, armed only with pistols and petrol bombs, tried to halt them. In the desperate battle that followed, the Germans destroyed the entire ghetto with fire and bombs, killing 5,000 Jews.

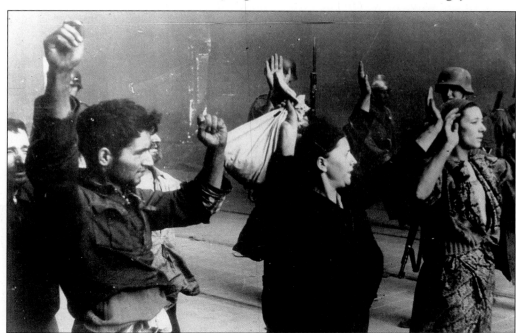

Source 6

Jewish resistance fighters captured by SS troops during the Warsaw Ghetto uprising in April 1943.

Questions

1   Study Source 4. What can you tell from it about the conditions inside the camp at Auschwitz?

2   Using Source 5 for information, explain why prisoners rarely rebelled against such awful conditions.

3   The Jews in Source 6 were poorly armed and few in number. Why then did they risk fighting the well-armed Germans?

4   Using the sources and information on pages 76–81 and 112–115, explain why it was possible for the Nazis to kill six million Jewish people.

The German Home Front

Hitler and the Nazis were in power for twelve and a half years. For almost six of those years, Germany was at war. How did this affect the people of Germany?

How did the war affect German civilians?

Shortages and rationing

As you have read (page 86) many things were in short supply even before the war began. This was because Germany was cutting imports from other countries in order to be self-sufficient.

When the war started, Germany was able to make up some shortages by taking goods from the countries it conquered. But many of the shortages continued and some grew worse. Sources 1 and 2 illustrate two of the ways in which the government tried to overcome the problem.

Source 1

A week's rations for one person in Germany: 2.4 kg of bread, 3.5 kg of potatoes, 250 g of meat, 185 g of fats (including powdered milk shown here made up with water), 60 g of cheese, 175 g of jam, half an egg, 150 g of cereal, 60 g of coffee.

Source 2

Heinrich Hauser, *Hitler Versus Germany. A Survey of Present-Day Germany from the Inside*, 1940.

* **Four-Year Plan** The plan for developing the economy started in 1936 (see page 86). It continued into the war even when the four years were over.

The German citizen, after shaving in the morning, puts the used blade in a small savings box, because Goering requires steel for the Four-Year Plan*.

The German housewife carefully places kitchen refuse in a special steel container.... She knows that this refuse will be collected to be used as fodder in a new piggery established by the city government....

Every week, groups of Hitler Youth – one week boys and the next week girls – go from house to house to collect waste from the 'Raw Materials Saving Boxes' – empty food-cans, tinfoil, and old newspapers. With handbarrows they march to the outskirts of towns and villages and pick over dump heaps for old pots, kitchen ranges, rusty buckets and bed frames....

Source 3

This photograph, taken from an aeroplane, shows the city of Cologne after more than a thousand British aircraft dropped bombs on it in the 'Thousand Bomber Raid' on 30 May 1942. In this one raid, 486 people were killed and 58,000 homes were destroyed.

Bombing

From the start of the war in 1939 the British Royal Air Force made bombing raids on Germany. At first they attacked only military targets. In 1940 they also tried to bomb industrial targets such as factories and oil refineries. But these targets were hard to find and hard to hit. From 1942 onwards, therefore, the RAF Bomber Command bombed whole towns and cities rather than just military or industrial targets. Sources 3 and 4 give some idea of how civilians were affected by the bombing.

Source 4

Jacob Schultz, a citizen of Darmstadt, recalling a British air raid on the city in 1944 in Klaus Schmidt, *Die Brandnacht* ('The Night of Fire'), 1965.

There were no windows in the trains, no schools, no doctors, no post, no telephone. One felt completely cut off from the world. To meet a friend who had survived was a wonderful experience. There was no water, no light, no fire. A candle was of priceless value. Little children collected wood from the ruins for cooking. Every family dug its own latrine in the garden.

Refugees

The bombing of Germany's cities made millions of people homeless. Many of these became refugees, leaving their home towns to look for refuge elsewhere.

The biggest movement of refugees took place in the closing stages of the war in 1945. By then, sixteen million Germans lived in occupied Eastern Europe, in areas like western Poland. As the Soviet armies advanced west in 1945 many of them fled in panic. They were terrified by thoughts of what would happen to them if they were captured. After the war's end, millions more were expelled from Poland, Czechoslovakia, Hungary and other countries liberated from Nazi rule. They were transported in appalling conditions to Germany. Out of sixteen million refugees in 1945, around two million died of cold, hunger, disease and exhaustion.

Source 5

A family of refugees, carrying their possessions in bags, boxes and a baby's pram, hurry through a bombed-out street in 1945. The child is holding a white flag of surrender.

Questions

1 Look at Source 3.
   a What did the bombing raid do to (i) the streets, (ii) buildings, (iii) bridges, (iv) docks in Cologne?
   b In what ways was this likely to affect the people of Cologne?

2 What other effects of bombing raids can you find in Source 4?

3 Using Sources 1–5 as evidence, make a list of ways in which German civilians were affected by war.

Hitler's German opponents

As you have read, the Nazis did not allow opposition. Communists, Jehovah's Witnesses, or anyone else who disagreed with them, were put into concentration camps. Between 1933 and 1945, some three million Germans saw the inside of a concentration camp. But the Nazis could not destroy all their opponents. A small number escaped arrest and did their best to overthrow Hitler. They were most active during the war years.

Left-wing opposition

On the left wing, dozens of small resistance groups gave help to the Soviet Union. The Red Orchestra, for example, was a spy network that passed military information to the Soviet army. The biggest left-wing group, led by Anton Saefkow (see Source 3) carried out sabotage, organised strikes, and encouraged soldiers to desert from the army.

Conservative opposition

On the right wing was the Kreisau Circle, consisting of officers and aristocrats, academics and professional people. At secret meetings in the town of Kreisau, they worked out a plan for governing Germany by democratic and Christian principles after Hitler had been overthrown.

Youth opposition

Thousands of young people started to oppose the Nazis during the war years. As you have read, many showed their opposition by joining groups such as the Edelweiss Pirates or the Navajos (see Source 1).

The most active young opponents were a group of Munich University students known as the White Rose. Led by Hans and Sophie Scholl and Christoph Probst (see Source 2), this group worked against the Nazis by distributing leaflets, putting up posters and writing graffiti on walls.

Source 1

A group of Navajos in 1940. The picture appeared in a manual for use by the police describing the different kinds of rebel youth groups. The caption describes them as a 'Wild Clique from Cologne'.

Wilde Clique aus Köln (Ostern 1940)

Source 2

The leaders of the White Rose group, Hans Scholl (left), Sophie Scholl (centre), and Christoph Probst. They were arrested and executed in 1944.

Assassins

Most of Hitler's opponents wanted him dead. Some were prepared to kill him. From 1935 onwards, assassins tried to shoot him or blow him up on at least eleven occasions. Every attempt failed, twice because Hitler did not keep to his expected schedule and once because a bomb failed to explode.

Hitler came closest to being killed in July 1944 when a group of army officers planned to take over the government. Their bomb, which exploded under a table at which Hitler was standing, injured but did not kill him. In the confusion that followed, the officers did not carry out their plans quickly enough, allowing the Gestapo to arrest the leaders. Thousands of conspirators were later rounded up and many were executed.

What were the aims of Hitler's opponents?

Very few of Hitler's opponents survived. All too often they were arrested by the Gestapo and tortured into revealing the names of other conspirators. Mass arrests were then followed by trials for treason in which the sentence was usually death. So why did so many Germans risk torture and death to oppose Hitler? What were they trying to achieve?

There isn't much evidence to help us answer that question. Much of the written evidence was destroyed by the Gestapo, and few opponents survived to tell their tale. Source 3 is an example of the kind of evidence that is available. It is from the last will and testament of the Communist resister, Anton Saefkow, who was arrested by the Gestapo in 1944. He wrote it in prison, shortly before being executed, with pencil and paper secretly obtained by his fellow prisoners. Each then memorised a paragraph before destroying the document. At the end of the war they got together and reconstructed the text from memory. The main points were:

Source 3

Quoted in Michael Balfour, *Withstanding Hitler in Germany, 1933–45*, 1988.

* **fascism** As used here, this is another word for Nazism.

1 Root out Fascism*. ...
2 The factories are to be taken over by the workers, who must have the power to make decisions and give orders....
3 Allow only a single union and have only one branch in each factory.
4 Build the new Germany on people's committees.
5 The future belongs to the working class....

Many resistance groups used leaflets to spread their ideas. This was dangerous work and many resisters were arrested with their leaflets. However, enough leaflets survived the war to be a useful source of evidence. Source 4 is an extract from a leaflet of the White Rose group.

Source 4

White Rose leaflet number 3, written in 1942, quoted in Inge Scholl, *Six Against Tyranny*, 1955.

...Everyone has a right to an honest and workable government which guarantees the freedom of the individual and ensures the property of all.... Our present 'state' is a dictatorship of evil....Why do you not rise up...? Sabotage armaments and war industry plants; sabotage meetings, festivals, organisations, anything which National Socialism has created. Hinder the smooth operation of the war machine....

Source 5 is taken from the script of a radio broadcast that was never made. It was written by the bomb plotters who tried to kill Hitler on 20 July 1944. They planned to broadcast it the day after Hitler's death, when they had taken over the government.

Source 5

Quoted in Fabian von Schlabrendorff, *The Secret War Against Hitler*, 1966.

Hitler had only contempt for truth and right. In place of truth he put propaganda; in place of right violence. Propaganda and the Gestapo were his means of staying in power. For him, only one ultimate value existed: the state.... Man was to be no more than a part, member and functionary of the state....

In place of this...the new Reichs Government will establish a state in accordance with the Christian traditions of the Western World, and based on the principles of civic duty, loyalty, service, and achievement for the common good, as well as respect for the individual and his natural rights as a human being.

Questions

1   **a** How was Source 3 written and recorded?
   b Why do you think Anton Saefkow's fellow prisoners recorded his ideas in this way?
   c Does this method of recording affect the usefulness of Source 1 as evidence of Anton Saefkow's aims? Explain your answer.

2   What criticisms of Nazism are made in Sources 4 and 5?

3   **a** Look at Source 1. These young people did not try to spread their ideas as the students in Source 2 did. Judging by this photograph only, how did they show their opposition to Nazism?
   b Suggest why the Nazis found this form of opposition so worrying.

Defeat and 'denazification'

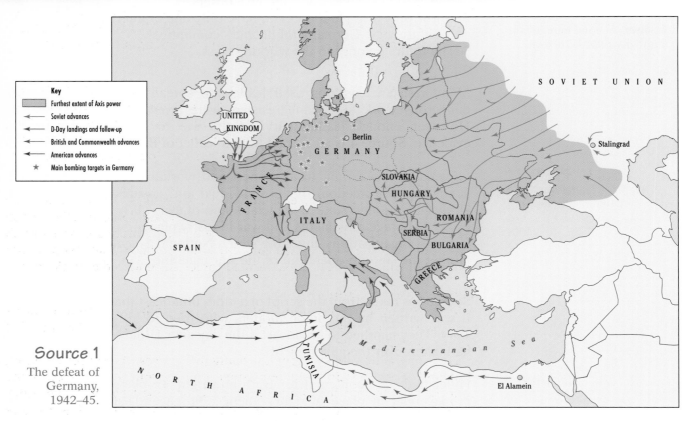

Source 1

The defeat of Germany, 1942–45.

As Source 1 shows, the Germans had occupied much of Europe by the end of 1942. But the more land they occupied, the more they had to defend and control. This became increasingly difficult from 1943 onwards.

The Russian Front

The Germans' greatest difficulties were in the Soviet Union. Despite occupying all of the west of the country in 1941, they could not defeat the Soviet armies. After losing a year-long battle for control of Stalingrad, they started to retreat in February 1943. Further defeats throughout 1943 forced them out of the Soviet Union in 1944.

The Mediterranean war

German forces also faced difficulties in the Mediterranean region. Their problems started in 1941 when they went to help the Italians fight the British in North Africa. Although they forced the British to retreat, the Germans could not defeat them. Then, in October 1942, they were themselves forced to retreat after losing the Battle of Alamein.

Meanwhile, the USA had joined the war on Britain's side. American forces now arrived in North Africa and halted the German retreat in Tunisia. The Germans and Italians surrendered in May 1943.

Next, the British and American Allies invaded Italy, forcing the Italians to surrender in July 1943. The Germans, fighting alone in Italy, slowly retreated north towards their own frontier.

The D-Day landings

The Germans came under attack from a third direction when the Allies invaded northern France on 6 June 1944 – code-named D-Day. In heavy fighting from June to September, two million Allied soldiers forced the Germans to retreat to their own frontier. An Allied invasion of southern France, Operation Anvil, prevented them from escaping southwards.

The bomber offensive

Meanwhile, Germany itself was being attacked from the air. From 1942 onwards British aircraft, later joined by American aircraft, made 'area bombing' raids on hundreds of towns and cities. Nearly half a million civilians were killed. Three million homes were destroyed. Factories, mines, power stations and transport centres were put out of action.

Surrender

Under attack from south, east and west, as well as from the air, the Germans could not hope to win the war. The end came in 1945 when Soviet troops entered eastern Germany while the Americans and British advanced from the west. When they captured Berlin in May 1945, Hitler committed suicide. The German armed forces surrendered a week later.

The division of Germany

After defeating Germany, the Allies set about ridding the country of its Nazi past. Their aims were to destroy Nazi power and to make sure that Germany could never fight again.

Their first action was to split Germany into pieces. As Source 2 shows, East and West Prussia were put under Polish control. The rest of the country was divided into four zones, each occupied by an Allied army. Berlin, the capital, was likewise split into four sectors. Austria was separated from Germany and also put under four-power occupation.

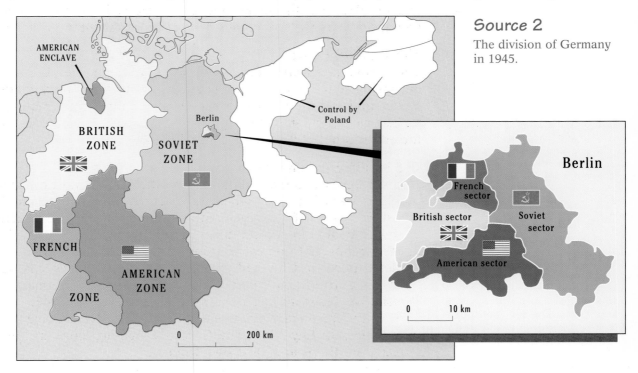

Source 2

The division of Germany in 1945.

Source 3

A painting of the Nuremberg Trial of 1946–47 by British artist Dame Laura Knight. As an official war artist she was present at the trial and painted the lawyers (left), prisoners (centre) and military policemen (right) from life. She added the scenes of devastation in the background from her imagination.

The punishment of war criminals

In the four occupation zones, as well as in countries freed from Nazi rule, thousands of Nazi officials were arrested and put on trial for crimes committed in the war.

The most important of the Nazis were tried by an Inter-Allied Special Tribunal at Nuremberg between 1945 and 1947. The main trial involved 21 top Nazi party leaders (see Source 3). Ten were hanged and the others imprisoned for 'crimes against peace and humanity'. Thousands of lesser Nazis were tried for similar crimes in the years that followed.

Denazification

Next, the Allies declared the Nazi Party illegal. Thousands of former Nazis were expelled from important state posts. In an attempt to make sure that nobody was overlooked, millions of Germans were made to fill out detailed questionnaires about their past. In the American zone alone, thirteen million questionnaires were completed. These revealed that some three million people had a Nazi background.

Re-education

Equally thorough efforts were made to 'denazify' the German education system. Millions of school books containing Nazi ideas were destroyed and new textbooks hurriedly rewritten. Nazi teachers were sacked or retrained. Schools started teaching a new, non-Nazi curriculum. Hundreds of thousands of prisoners of war were 're-educated' in specially created colleges before being returned to Germany.

To back up this 're-education' of the German people, the Allied authorities took control of the German press, radio and films, and made sure they put across democratic instead of Nazi ideas.

Did denazification work?

Denazification proved to be more difficult than the Allies expected. One problem was finding non-Nazis to replace the Nazis who were expelled from government jobs. Saul Padover, an American soldier in Germany in 1945, described some of the non-Nazis who took over from expelled Nazis in the city of Aachen:

Source 4

From the diary of Saul K.Padover, *Psychologist in Germany*, 1946.

* **clichés** Over-used sayings or expressions.

> Their strong point…is that they are 'anti-Nazi' or 'non-Nazi'. Their proof is that they never joined the Party.
>
> (But) these men are not democratic-minded. They profess a marked distaste for the Weimar Republic…. In varying degrees and tones, one or other repeats the clichés* of the Nazis – that Germany was dishonoured by the Versailles Treaty, that the latter was too harsh, that…Germany was betrayed when the Fourteen Points were not kept, that the 'poor Reich'…must expand.

The re-education of schoolchildren was especially difficult. While the Allies were able to destroy all Nazi textbooks, they did not have the resources to write new ones themselves. The writing of new textbooks was therefore left to the Germans. In the case of history, this did not always produce the results which the Allies intended. Source 5 is an example of the problem. Taken from a school textbook on recent history published in 1958, it is *all* that was said about Jews in Nazi Germany.

Source 5

Ernst Klett, *Geschichte der Neuesten Zeit* ('A History of Recent Times'), 1958.

In November 1938 there occurred an especially shameful event. An emigrated Jew shot a German diplomat in Paris, who had been anything but an enemy of the Jews. This deed was excessively exaggerated by the Nazis and used as an excuse for a vigorous persecution of the Jews. By the orders of Goebbels the members of different organisations of the Party burned the synagogues. They also mistreated many Jews and damaged the Jewish stores more or less severely.

The basic problem about re-education was described in a talk given in 1985 by Michael Balfour. He had been the Chief of Information Services in the British zone of Germany from 1945 to 1947.

Source 6

Michael Balfour, *In Retrospect: Britain's Policy of Re-education*, 1985.

I still wish we could have been more active but by now I doubt whether it would have done much good. The frame of mind of Germans in the closing months of the war is a fascinating subject.... 30 per cent of them retained their faith in Hitler till very near the end. The proportion of those professing to think Nazism 'a good thing badly carried out' never dropped below 42 per cent between November 1945 and January 1948. There is good evidence that 10 per cent of the adult male population remained convinced Nazis – 4 million people....

Questions

1   Look at Source 3
   a Dame Laura Knight painted this trial scene from observation. Why do you think she added the imaginary background scenes?
   b The background scenes make the painting more than a portrait of the trial. It is an artist's interpretation of events. Which events in the war do you think support her interpretation?

2   Read Source 5 carefully.
   a Now turn back to page 77 and read the paragraph headed 'The Night of Broken Glass'. It describes the same events as Source 5. How do the two accounts differ?
   b Use the index of this book to find references to Jews in Nazi Germany. Make a list of events concerning Jews in Nazi Germany which are not mentioned in Source 5.
   c Why can Source 5 be criticised as an historical account of Jews in Nazi Germany?

3   In Source 6, Michael Balfour said he wished the Allies had been 'more active' in the 're-education' of Germans but thought it would not have done much good.
   a Judging by Sources 4–6, why do you think he thought this would not have done much good?
   b Despite these difficulties, suggest what more the Allies could have done to 're-educate' Germany.

Unit 8 Review

In 1977 a German journalist, Dieter Bossman, interviewed senior school students in German schools to find out what they knew about Hitler. The following extracts from the interviews are typical examples of what they told him.

Dieter Bossman (ed.), *Was ich über Adolf Hitler gehört habe* ('What I have heard about Adolf Hitler'), 1977.

Kirsten, age 16: Adolf Hitler was himself a Jew and was mocked by everyone.

Otto, age 16: He freed Germany of the Jews. In all the larger businesses there was a Jew. The Germans were oppressed.

Ute, age 16: Concentration camps were later constructed where the Jews were gassed. The Jews were warned long beforehand, however, and told they should emigrate.

Hubertus, age 19: In order to get a pure race, they didn't have to resort to concentration camps right away. He could certainly have thought of something that was not so 'gruesome'. Surely he could have given out Jewish expulsions from the Reich.

Thomas, age 15: He ordered that all Jews on the streets after 8 o'clock would simply be shot. (The worst thing was that they didn't have watches.)

Joachim, age 18: The Jews had to be removed. Since no one wanted to admit them, not even Roosevelt* who was a Jew, they had to be killed.

Renate, age 15: I think about the Jews. He surely could have found another way to kill them.

Thomas, age 17: Hitler had the Jews killed because he wanted to have only Germans in his Empire.

* **Roosevelt** The President of the USA, 1933–45.

Questions

1 **a** What was it that all these young people had heard about Hitler?
  b How might this be explained?

2 How do these statements suggest that young Germans in the 1970s knew very little about Hitler and the Nazis?

3 **a** Select one statement that you think shows a lack of historical understanding.
  b Explain what you consider wrong about it.

4 Are these statements evidence that the denazification of Germany after 1945 failed? Explain your answer.

5 **a** Make a list of things which you think young people, whether in Germany or any other country, should learn about Hitler and the Nazis before leaving school.
  b Explain why you think they should know about these things.

Index

Numbers in *italics* refer to pictures